The Virgin Islands Illustrated
Illustrated
A Sailing Odyssey

D1532360

The Virgin Islands Illustrated
A Sailing Odyssey

by
David and Nancy Harris

Tortuga  Books
Summerland Key, Florida

Top Cat

For Claire, Dan, and Ken

The Virgin Islands Illustrated
A Sailing Odyssey

TORTUGA BOOKS
P.O. Box 420564
Summerland Key, FL 33042

Publisher's Cataloguing-in-Publication
(Provided by Quality Books, Inc.)

Harris, David (David Ernest), 1942-
  The Virgin Islands Illustrated : a sailing odyssey / by David and Nancy Harris. -- 1st ed.
  p. cm.
  Includes index.
  LCCN: 99-61551
  ISBN: 1-893561-02-X

  1. Harris, David (David Ernest), 1942- -- Journeys. 2. Harris, Nancy Jane, 1944- -- Journeys. 3. Sailing--Virgin Islands. 4. Virgin Islands-- Description and travel. I. Harris, Nancy Jane, 1944- II. Title.

F2006.H37 1999   917.297'204
            QBI99-254

Contents

4: Salt Island to Virgin Gorda

5: Anegada

6: The Baths and Trellis Bay

7: Going to the Dogs

8: Road Town

9: Back in the USVI

Exploring the waters of Great Thatch — To Soper's Hole for lunch — How do you say "Pusser's"? — Checking out of the British Virgins — Flocking tourists at Cruz Bay — The Park Service visitor center   **118**

10: St. Croix

A bumpy trip over—Anchorage at Christiansted Harbor — Touring Fort Christeansvaern — A charming downtown — Setting off by rental car — Beautiful St. George Botanical Garden — A K-Mart with a difference! — Renovations at Fort Frederik — The wood workshop of St. Croix Leap — Glorious coastal vistas — A short sail to Buck Island National Monument — Circling the island by dinghy — Snorkeling the reef — A trail to the summit — The anchorage clears out — Snorkeling the near-in shallows — To Salt River Bay — Where Columbus landed — Hurricane damage — Nesting egrets   **124**

11: Back to St. John

Big seas en route to St. John — A hike to Ram Head, with a spectacular view — Snorkeling in Trunk Bay — To Leinster Bay — The Annaberg Sugar Mill ruins — Snorkeling around Waterlemon Cay — A determined sailboarder — Donkey serenades and bird songs   **158**

12: Sailing Around St. Thomas

Thatch palms at Mary's Point — Into the Windward Passage — Squeezing between Congo Cay and Lovango Cay — Across the Leeward Passage — Lunch in Magens Bay — The western side of St. Thomas — Capella and Buck Islands — Right back where we started from   **172**

Afterword   **184**

Index   **186**

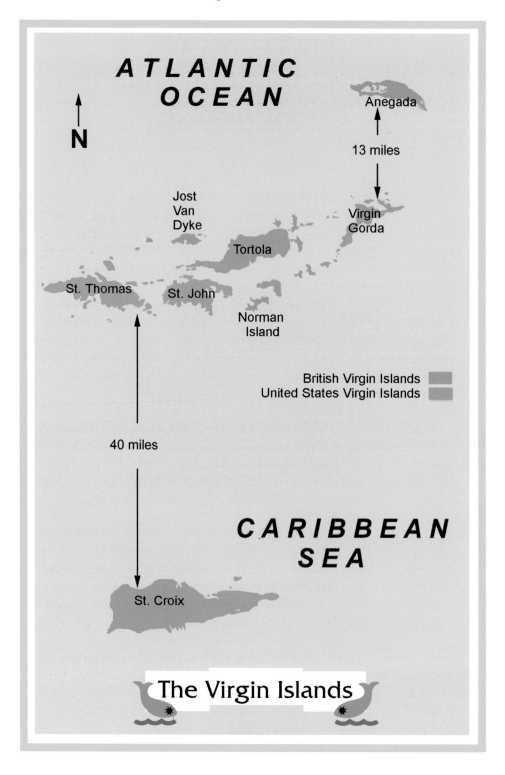

Introduction

Our boat, *Top Cat,* is a 32-foot catamaran sailboat manufactured by PDQ Yachts, Inc. in Whitby, Canada. We owned the boat for several years before we had the courage to even consider a cruise like the one described in this book. Our first trip was bringing *Top Cat* from Canada to a slip in Fort Pierce, Florida, and quite an adventure it was, too, for people who had never owned or sailed anything larger than a small daysailor. The following summer we traveled around Florida, from Port Salerno on the east coast around Cape Sable at the southernmost tip of the peninsula and then up the west coast to the panhandle, and then across Florida by canal back home. We made other, shorter trips to the keys west of Key West, the Thousand Islands area on Florida's west coast, and the islands of Florida Bay.

These trips didn't supply enough excitement for David, who longed for more adventure at sea — a real voyage! It was decided that he would sail the boat alone to the Virgin Islands (a trip chronicled in his book, *Sailing Through Paradise: The Illustrated Adventures of a Single-handed Sailor).* On his arrival, Nancy would fly down to join him in the Virgin Islands for a month.

Things slowly fell into place. Our older son agreed to look after our younger one for the month when both of us would be gone. David made the necessary boat upgrades for a long cruise and purchased and stowed provisions for many months at sea. To-do lists were made and items checked off as tasks were completed. Ready at last, *Top Cat* loaded with food and other supplies for months at sea, David departed early in the morning on the first day of spring in 1998.

Nancy wondered and worried as David journeyed toward his goal. He called home every week or so to describe his progress (rapid) and problems (numerous, but fortunately not unsolvable). He arrived safely in St. Thomas, much to Nancy's relief, and she flew down to join him the following week.

Living aboard a boat, for those who have never done it, takes some getting used to. We've developed a thrifty and relatively simple lifestyle on *Top Cat.* The following is a brief explanation of how we manage the necessities of daily life while cruising.

Food.   With a refrigerator capable of producing enough ice cubes for our evening gin-and-tonics and keeping canned drinks cold, and a two-burner stovetop for boiling water for morning coffee and making simple hot meals, our little galley is perfectly adequate. Breakfast is usually cold fruit juice (from a box) and cereal with Parmalat, milk with a long storage life that comes in boxes, and hot coffee or tea. Lunch consists of sandwiches and raw veg-etables or fruit, or both, whatever we can buy locally, and canned soda or ice tea. Supper is a hot meal of canned stew, chili, spaghetti, ravioli, or any one of a number of combinations of canned vegetables, meats, sauces, pasta, and rice. While in the Virgin Islands, we enjoyed many restaurant meals. We preferred eating out for lunch, since we liked to be aboard the boat to watch the sun set and talk over the events of the day in peace and privacy.

View of the galley, looking forward from the port cabin

Washing up. We refill the boat's 47-gallon water tank whenever we stop at a marina for gas. We prefer, however, not to have to stop very often, and our boat uses little enough gas so we don't have to. On our Virgin Islands trip we had a large number of water containers that held between a liter and ten gallons of additional water. We kept a topless 12-gallon plastic cooler lashed under the corner of the boat's hardtop to catch rainwater. We washed dishes in saltwater scooped from the sea in a bucket and then dried them quickly with a dishtowel. David took seawater baths, jumping in and soaping up, then rinsing off under the spray of water from one of the shower bags. Nancy scrubbed down in the cockpit of the boat using a bucket of saltwater, then rinsed off with fresh water from a shower bag. We both wore clothing that could be washed by hand and hung out to dry on the lifelines around the deck. We also used marina laundramats.

Waste disposal. Empty metal cans and glass jars and bottles can be dumped at sea (we crush aluminum cans flat and fill other cans and glass containers with water so they will sink), but plastic, paper, and other trash must be collected in plastic trash bags and disposed of at marinas or town dumpsters, whatever is available where we are. Some cruisers burn paper trash, but we have never done the kind of cruising in which we couldn't find a trash receptacle somewhere along our route, even if we had to hang onto bags of trash for a week. Our marine head, which flushes with saltwater pumped out of the sea, empties into a 30-gallon holding tank that we empty when we're outside the 3-mile limit.

Energy. *Top Cat* has two 9.9-horsepower Yamaha engines. They produce electrical energy that is stored in two batteries for later use. Engine-generated electricity is supplemented with energy from solar panels mounted on the hardtop and between the davits, which hold the dinghy, at the boat's stern. The refrigerator, stovetop, and oven use propane, which is replenished with some difficulty. First we must find a place that sells propane, then we must take the tanks ashore on the dinghy and haul them to the propane dealer, then we must haul them back. Needless to say, we are economical in our use of propane. Foods that require long periods of stovetop cooking or the use of the oven are seldom on our menu. (One great discovery we made during this cruise is coffee bags. Like teabags, they require only hot water. The coffee is as good as perked, which takes more propane to prepare.) As for lighting, we adapt our daily routine to the movement of the sun through the sky. When we're cruising we get up at dawn and go to bed not more than an hour or two after sunset. We usually have an anchor light or two on at night to keep other boats from ramming us in the darkness. We also have small cabin fans that furnish a breeze and white noise for a restful night's sleep.

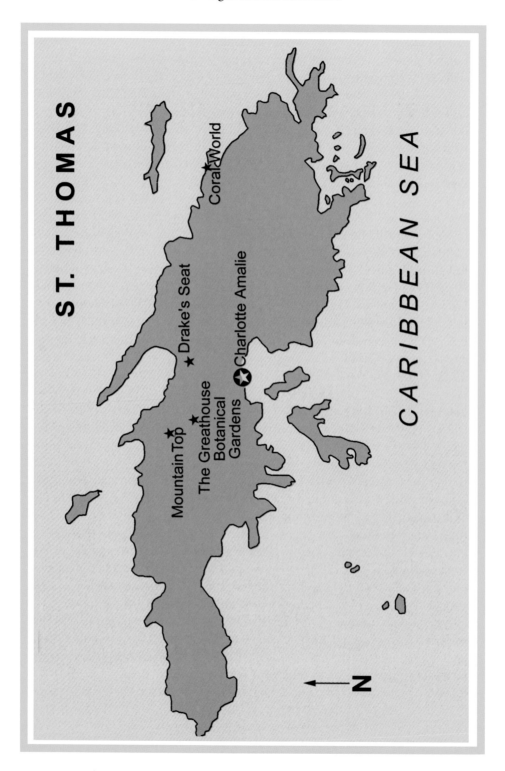

1: Sightseeing in St. Thomas

Charlotte Amalie (say ah – MALL – yuh), the capital of St. Thomas, is the point of entry in the Virgin Islands for the airlines and cruise lines, and for us as well. Our catamaran sailboat, *Top Cat*, is docked at Crown Bay Marina in the town's naturally deep harbor, where we get a front-row seat for the loading of a big container ship nearby. The loading, which employs huge cranes that attach to cradles on the tops of the containers, goes on all day and all night long.

We pick up a rental car at the airport and begin our tour of the Virgin Islands by land with a drive through downtown Charlotte Amalie. It is Sunday afternoon. The many shops and stores catering to tourists are locked up behind pairs of sturdy double wooden doors; we are pleased to be able to look with-

...a drive through downtown Charlotte Amalie...

out the temptation to buy. Buildings in the oldest part of town date from the 1700s and 1800s, when the Danes owned the island. The streets here are old-town narrow, clearly never meant for two-way vehicular traffic. They have deep gutters on either side, built long ago to drain rainwater and wastewater. These old structures are an enduring tribute to Danish construction techniques. They have withstood floods and hurricanes, boom times and bad times. They are now part of history and are protected by law from demolition. They will not be torn down to make way for multi-story condos or office buildings. They have survived natural disasters and the human propensity to raze and rebuild. Their future is assured.

On Monday morning we head off in our rental car for a longer tour of the island. We expect to see most everything in a very short time, since St. Thomas is only about 15 miles long and 5 miles wide. This little island, like nearly all of those in the United States Virgin Islands (USVI) and British Virgin Islands (BVI), is described as "mountainous." At its highest point it rises about 1500 feet above sea level. Because of the hilly terrain, the roads are steep and winding, with sudden turns and gut-wrenching grades. The 10- and 20-mph speed limit signs seem desirable on these roads. In the Virgins, people drive on the left side of the road, though vehicles are mostly U.S. models with steering wheels on the left side. The tourist in a rental car, driving on the wrong side of a narrow, steep road with puny or nonexistent guardrails and sudden sharp curves, will be naturally cautious. Soon this cautious driver will be leading a parade of cars driven by much less cautious Virgin Islanders who will one by one cross the double yellow lines to pass at speeds far in excess of the limits posted. At least, that is our experience.

Our first stop is Drake's Seat, a concrete bench perched above the road. It marks the spot where Sir Francis Drake, who claimed the Virgin Islands for England, is said to have sat watching rival naval fleets sail in to dispute his claim. This is indeed a great perch for watching boats and for enjoying the view of Magens Bay, as well. Today's vista has a group of T-shirt peddlers in the foreground. We buy four T-shirts at a significantly reduced price, get back in the car, and continue our trip.

Our next stop is the World-Famous Mountaintop, a shopping mall on the mountainside. It is devoted to the tourist trade. We share a World-Famous banana daiquiri and enjoy another beautiful view from the veranda of the restaurant/bar. Then we go off to the shops to buy stuff, a souvenir plate, another T-shirt, an elephant carving (made in Indonesia and sticky with var-

...a great perch for...enjoying the view of Magens Bay...

nish), and a limited-edition print of colorful rowboats produced by a local artist. The shops in this tourist mall are spotless, elegant, and air-conditioned, and droves of other tourists are here with us, looking for a way to take some West Indies magic home.

Satisfied that we have done our bit for the island's economy, we get back in the car to continue our road tour. We visit Estate St. Peter Mountain Greathouse and Botanical Gardens. The name is longer than the associated experience, which consists of a stroll past several buildings via walkways and stairs to enjoy their setting of tropical plants, fountains, and pools. The gardens, we

... tropical plants, fountains, and pools.

learn, are under construction, being renovated. The price of a ticket includes unlimited drinks, a choice of neon-red non-alcoholic punch, neon-red rum punch, or icewater, a welcome offering on this warm day.

We take pictures of breadfruit on a breadfruit tree and admire the red torch gingers. We stalk a bananaquit and get a good photograph of this native Vir-

...and admire the red torch gingers.

gin Island bird — appropriately, in a banana tree, though we do not see it sipping nectar from the flower.

Outside, on the Greathouse's front lawn, we spot a very large lizard that reminds us again how different these islands are from the Keys. We've got nothing like this colorful creature back home.

...a bananaquit...in a banana tree...

...a very large lizard...

Next we head for Coral World, which provides an underwater view of a coral reef. It is currently also under renovation. We are turned away, disappointed.

By now we have completely circled the island and enjoyed many fantastic views of the St. Thomas shoreline and the harbor.

...many fantastic views...

...the harbor.

We have arrived back at Charlotte Amalie, where we tour Fort Christian, a small red building with the date 1671 tacked above its front gate. It appears to lack the wherewithal to deflect any sort of determined attack, unlike the massive forts we have visited in Florida and elsewhere that were built to guard seacoasts.

Fort Christian's many tiny rooms are filled with exhibits, including the works of local artists and the history of the islands in text and illustrations. We are intrigued by the wooden structure in the courtyard inside. It looks at first glance like an instrument of torture, but then we read the plaque next to it: "The long poles run from the animals' harness to the center shaft which turns the rollers. Juice comes down the trough to vats." It is a sugarcane press!

..we tour Fort Christian...

...a good view of the harbor...

We climb to the fort's flat roof. From there we have a good view of the harbor and we can look out on a cluster of tents where street vendors sell souvenirs and treats to milling tourists. We are finished with shopping, however, and when we leave the fort, we climb into our rental car and search out a local market where we can do some provisioning.

While food is expensive, everything we need is available here, and more. We are puzzled by the large displays of packets of unfamiliar spices and other dry goods throughout the store. Many packets are marked with their use. Several are used together to make something called "Irish moss drink." One kind, marked "chew sticks," looks like, well, sticks. Our marketing and land tour

...a cluster of tents where street vendors sell souvenirs...

over, we turn in our car, thinking about the adventures that lie ahead. Driving around St. Thomas has been fun, but tomorrow we will continue our explorations by more appropriate means.

Tomorrow we sail!

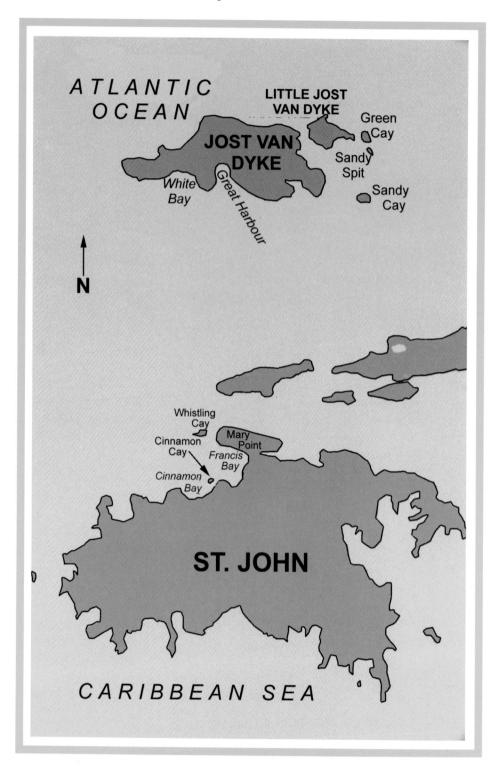

2: St. John and Jost Van Dyke

In the morning, aboard *Top Cat*, we depart the bustling marina for a quiet anchorage in Cinnamon Bay, at Virgin Islands National Park which is administered by the U.S. National Park Service on St. John. St. John is a short hop, hardly worth raising the sails. On St. John we find the locales featured in the Virgins advertisements: white crescent beaches bordering turquoise seas, lush vegetation carpeting the mountain slopes beyond. We snorkel around Cinnamon Cay, a rocky islet in the bay. Rocks big and small, from Volkswagen boulders to breadloaf-sized chunks, form the backdrop for exotic sea life, spiny black sea urchins, round brain corals, sea fans in shades of purple and yellow, and fish in orange, powder blue, velvet black, yellow. Schools of tiny fish swirl around us like clusters of silver sparks.

...shiny black bees...

After lunch we move *Top Cat* from Cinnamon Bay to Francis Bay, a voyage of about a mile. We anchor again in sand, but here the water is only 15 feet deep and we are much closer to shore, making for a better and quieter anchorage. We dinghy in for a walk on Francis Bay Trail, one of the dozen or so trails maintained by the park. This trail is short, and goes uphill to some of the plantation ruins that dot the island, then downhill to a salt pond, a shallow, inland saltwater pond.

The trail takes us past tangled heaps of vines bright with pink flowers. The flowers have attracted numerous shiny black bees of the bumble variety, giants, bigger than any we've ever seen before. We circle a salt pond in which a black-necked stilt strolls along through the water on long pink legs. We reboard our dinghy to explore the coastline by sea. The unexpected is just around the corner: a donkey walking slowly along a rocky shoreline, grazing on clumps of vegetation along the way.

...a black-necked stilt strolls along through the water...

Guidebooks describe the origin of the donkeys and goats that inhabit the Virgins in such abundance. Hundreds of years ago, their ancestors were brought here by the Danes. These domesticated animals provided milk, meat, and labor on the Danish sugarcane plantations. When the plantations shut down and the Danes left, the livestock remained behind, went wild, and prospered. Today most of the larger islands have feral populations of goats and donkeys.

Later, we take a dinghy tour of Whistling Cay off Mary Point at the west edge of Francis Bay. We see a naked man on a boat. Tourist brochures warn that there are no nude beaches and that going topless is not customary here, but we discover that many people ignore these admonitions and do as pretty much as they wish, especially when they are aboard their boats.

Night arrives with an altogether new show. The lights of St. Thomas, only a few miles away, glitter like stars scattered across the island's dark slopes.

The next morning, we set out for Great Harbour on Jost (say YOHST) Van Dyke, British territory. On our way in we pass a spectacular four-masted schooner, surely the largest sailing ship in these waters.

...a spectacular, four-masted schooner...

We anchor in the deep harbor and dinghy through a channel in the reef to a dinghy dock. We are here only to check in at immigration and customs, both located in a small white building at the end of the dock. Inside, the office is crowded with people waiting to clear customs.

The customs man gives us pens and we fill out forms, two for immigration and one for customs. We exchange information. No, we have no weapons aboard. No, the customs man has no mooring permits to sell. We must go to one of the other ports of entry for a mooring permit, either Road Harbor on Tortola, or West End on Jost Van Dyke, to buy a BVI mooring permit. We would very much like to buy a mooring permit. It would give us the chance to tie up to a mooring instead of having to anchor. These waters are crowded with boats and their great depth often makes anchoring a challenge. In USVI waters, it's first-come, first-served, and it's not necessary to pay for our moorings, but in the BVI, we must first buy a permit to use a public mooring. Private moorings are available, too, we discover, usually for a price, marked right on the mooring buoy, from $15 to $20 per night.

...we ...follow a rocky trail up the hill...

We are finished with customs, but the immigration officer is not in. We are told to return to the office in half an hour, so we take a walk along the beach to the west of the jetty in Great Harbour. At the western end we follow a rocky trail up the hill, from which we can look back and see the water.

We return to the office in half an hour for our immigration processing. The lady who serves us wears a crisp a black-and-white uniform with epaulettes like her customs counterpart. As she reviews our forms, she looks up, annoyed, and calls through the shuttered windows of her office to a man smoking outside in the island sunshine, "Please move away, the smoke is bothering me!" We can't help but smile. Definitely a no-nonsense lady.

She is cheerful despite the smoke, and efficiently processes us through. She needs 20 cents, but we have nothing smaller than a dollar bill.

"Have you no silver?" she asks, in a voice full of music. She steps out of her office to request change for our dollar bill from the milling, waiting tourists. U.S. currency is the money used everywhere in the BVI, a reflection of the fact that most of the visitors are Americans. We get our change and our transaction is complete. We are now legally in British territory, squared away for a visit of many weeks.

The immigration official has told us that she just checked in another *Top Cat*. We see it on our way out of the harbor. It is a catamaran powerboat, much smaller than our sailboat, but very much faster. It is out of sight in a flash while we move at our usual slow but stately pace out of Great Harbor.

Our next destination is White Bay, just one bay over, a distance of less than a mile, and we do not bother to raise our sails. We motor through the break in the reef marked by red and green buoys. We anchor in 10 feet of water off a beautiful sandy beach, where we find the Soggy Dollar Bar, "Home of the Painkiller." (The Painkiller is a rum drink, available everywhere in the Virgin Islands. To make a Painkiller, mix 1 1/2 ounces of dark rum, 1 ounce of orange juice, and 1 ounce of pineapple juice and pour over ice cubes, not crushed ice. Sprinkle with grated nutmeg. Having tasted this concoction, however, we suggest two aspirin instead — or a large gin and tonic.)

At the Soggy Dollar's open-air restaurant, we ignore the drink menu and order sandwiches of flying fish and spicy chicken breast, and a beer for each of us, which puts us in a cheerful frame of mind. This really is a pretty spot with

...White Bay...really is a pretty spot...

a curve of white sand fringed by coconut palms. The constant breeze makes it cool and the view is a picture postcard image of a tropical paradise. We walk the beach after lunch, and later snorkel the reef. The reef is mainly rock and dead corals, but we see many colorful tropical fish.

In the morning we pull up our anchor and head for Sandy Cay, a small island off the north end of Jost Van Dyke. Time for a hike. A very nice trail follows

...Sandy Cay, a small island off the north end of Jost Van Dyke.

its beach slightly inland, climbing to a tall cliff of rock at one end where the waves break noisily.

...a tall cliff of rock at one end where the waves break noisily...

On our way we encounter several softball-size nests hanging from the trees. Each nest is woven like a round basket of grass with a small round opening at the bottom for an entrance. These are the nests of bananaquits, which we see and hear everywhere around us. Bananaquits have a twittering call that sounds like an exaggerated, noisy, drawn-out kiss. They are tiny and very quick, and it's hard to follow the flickering travels of these birds, even as we reach the summit the island, where there's not much in the way of trees to hide them.

Each nest is woven like a round basket of grass...

We descend the hill and walk through the dense vegetation, passing a bush with fringelike blooms we later identify as a limber caper. The limber caper flower has four small white petals buried under a huge tuft of stamens. It looks as if it has experienced some kind of floral explosion.

...a limber caper...

Suddenly, we break free of the tropical forest. The trail emerges on the beach, where the sea seems impossibly bright and blue.

...the sea seems impossibly bright and blue.

We continue, strolling the white sandy beach. We come at last to the end of the sand, where the island's shore is rocky.   Here we watch crabs so nearly the same color as the rock we don't see them at first. They cling to the shore for dear life, hanging on each time a big wave washes over them. When a particularly large roller hits, we look to see if they have survived. Sometimes they appear to have moved a few inches but they do not get washed away. How this is managed, we cannot tell.   Perhaps they extend all eight legs in a death grip at the last moment, just before a wave breaks. We watch them for a long time and never do see them brace for impact.

...crabs...nearly the same color as the rocks...

Back on the beach, we move our chairs to the shade of a palm tree and have a lunch of sandwiches and soda. As we eat, we watch the passing scene. We discover that this is a very popular place for sunning, snorkeling, and boating. One by one, more boats come in and anchor. Dinghies ferry the boat passengers to shore where they spread towels or open folding chairs to relax on the sand. We are soon surprised to see that our private island has become crowded. Many vessels share our splendid anchorage.

The thrill is gone. We decide to move.

Many vessels now share our splendid anchorage.

We motor to Sandy Spit off Green Cay, about a mile away. Sandy Spit is a small island of coconut palms with an encircling beach and not much else. We discuss being shipwrecked on an island like this. We could eat coconuts and search for shellfish and other marine life to sustain us until our rescue, we conclude, but we would probably starve to death or die of thirst first.

We motor to Sandy Spit off Green Cay...

Sandy Spit is a small island of coconut palms...

We snorkel the reef between Sandy Spit and Green Cay. It is only two or three feet deep, and rocky, but there are some beautiful corals. It is hard to find a place that is not good snorkeling in these islands. We are already jaded. We take a dinghy trip between Green Cay and Little Jost Van Dyke past craggy rocks and blue, calm seas.

About 4 o'clock we pull up our anchor and leave for Cane Garden Bay on Tortola. We arrive in a crowded anchorage off a pretty white beach. Anchoring gives us a bit of trouble. When we put the anchor down and back off, we continue to move. We must be slipping. Is our anchor dragging? We have an exceptionally large and effective anchor attached to 40 feet of chain at the end of our rode. We can't be slipping! We dive on the anchor and discover that our chain has made a 90-degree turn around a big rock. The rock is being

...Cane Garden Bay...

moved by our chain, which pulls on it as we back the boat. The chain is straightening out as the rock moves, making it seem as if we are dragging the anchor. We move the boat forward and pull the chain over the rock. We back the boat and this time we hold firm.

We dinghy in for supper at a restaurant in Cane Garden Bay. There are several choices in the way of eateries and a nice long dinghy dock with lots of room left to accommodate our dinghy. The waitress at the place we choose does not seem happy to see us. Her first reaction to our arrival is to warn us off the reserved tables nearest the view of the bay. Later, she appears reluctant to fill our water glasses (ice, apparently, is only for drinks), and then to bring the bill. But the food, fried shrimp and lobster, is excellent, and we are hungry after a busy day of hiking and snorkeling.

After supper, we light our way with our flashlight down the long dinghy dock, tumble into our dinghy, and head for the boat and bed.

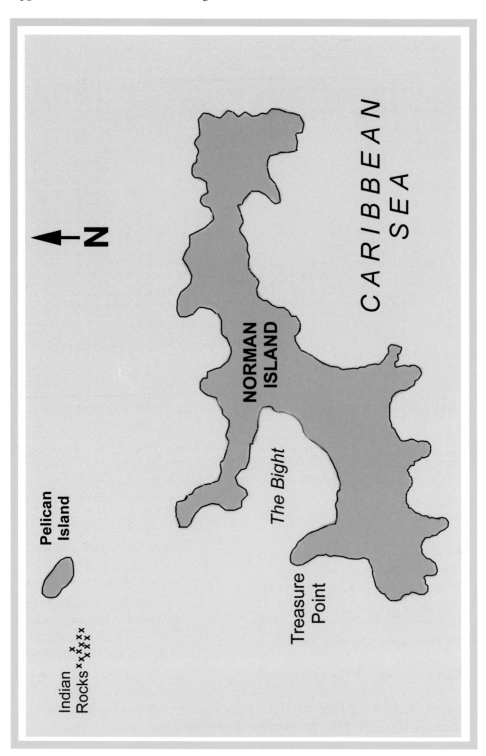

3: Norman Island

We leave early next morning for Norman Island and anchor in Norman Island Bight. At the innermost recesses of the Bight's sandy beach is a building whose roof is emblazoned with the name Billy Bones. A skull-and-crossbones flag flies over it. We learn that it is a beach bar tended by a fellow who likes the music turned *way, way up*. As a counterpoint to the incessant Caribbean beat provided by the bar's sound system, hammering and sawing noises accompany carpentry going on next door. A new building is rising on the remains of an ancient rock foundation, doubtless old plantation ruins.

...we dinghy over to Treasure Point to the world-famous caves ...

To escape the noise, we quickly gather up snorkel gear and dinghy over to Treasure Point to explore the sea caves. A dinghy mooring, a long bristly plastic line stretched between two floats secured to the sea bottom, offers a place to tie our dinghy when we are ready to snorkel.

...we paddle into the first large cave...

First, though, we turn off our motor and grab our paddles to explore the sea caves in *Catnap*, our dinghy. We paddle into the first large cave east of the point, the only one of the three large caves that will accommodate our tiny inflatable dinghy. It is longer than it first appears, perhaps a hundred feet, and it is wide enough inside for our boat to sneak through with a few inches clearance on both sides. There is no current, though surges from boat wakes jostle us as we move along. On the vaulted cave ceiling, where water drips down

...back toward the cave entrance...

from above, we see a brilliant green stain of algae the size of a dinner plate. Marine organisms, probably sponges, mark the rock walls in lavender and orange scrawls at the waterline. We go all the way to the end of the cave, examining the walls with our flashlight, then turn around and paddle back toward the cave entrance.

We leave the cave to discover that a boatload of tourists has just arrived and droves of snorkelers are spreading out over the water toward the caves.

We tie our dinghy up on the mooring line and put on our masks and fins. As snorkelers we investigate the underwater part of the cave we have just explored by boat. The rocks below the water's surface are coated with many kinds of encrusting corals, and fish drift beneath us into the darkness. We move on to a smaller, shallower cave west of the big one.

...fish drift beneath us into the darkness...

East of the biggest cave are two others. The first is shallow, with coral coatings of luminous hues. Here it is possible to climb out on the rocks, but undesirable, since it would damage the corals. The next cave is more complex. Once inside, you can turn left or right. Left trails off into darkness. Who knows what lies beyond? Right, and you climb over small rocks and out of the cave.

Satisfied that we have thoroughly explored the place, we take a dinghy tour along the shore. We glimpse a cluster of goats under a large and picturesque tree, and several signs, one warning of "broken slabs" (probably British for "loose rocks" and every bit as strange a phrase) and others boldly declaring "No Trespassing."

We will stay another day in the anchorage. We are glad to discover that Billy Bones Bar has run out of loud music for the moment. More boats pour in — long, sleek monohulls, a trimaran, many catamarans, all much larger vessels than ours. We erect our canvas shade over the front of the boat, hoping to catch some cool, and have drinks and then supper aboard.

...More boats pour in...

The next morning we make up our minds to look for a trail that goes uphill to the mountaintop, as described in the guidebook. We discover that it does not exist. Possibly the guidebook writer caught sight of some dry streambeds or goat paths on the hillside and simply assumed they constituted a trail. Possibly a trail did exist and it is now overgrown. No matter. There is no trail now. We break our own path through the brush and struggle to the top of the mountain. Along the way we meet a pearly-eyed thrasher, a bird we see as often in the Virgins as the bananaquit, but here is a calm bird, a quiet bird, a bird that will sit still for having its picture taken!

...a pearly-eyed thrasher...

From the top of the mountain, great views appear on all sides. We take pictures of Indian Rocks and Pelican Island on one side and of the boats anchored in Norman Island Bight on the other.

...Indian Rocks and Pelican Island...

...boats anchored in Norman Island Bight...

Later in the morning we dinghy out to Indian Rocks to snorkel. The seas are calm and the rocks only a five-minute dinghy ride away. We tie up at a mooring. The water is filled with divers; the snorkeling is excellent here. Some small rocks rise up out of the water. Fire coral grows in water so shallow that we must swim around, not over it, for fear of being stung. As at the caves, one attraction here is a nearly vertical rock wall covered with colorful marine life.

We return to the caves a few hours later to take some underwater pictures. We are surrounded by fish on several occasions at the caves, but now they seem more numerous than ever, surrounding swimmers in a mad whirl of silver. They crowd up too close, and we have to give up on taking pictures. Perhaps the custom is to feed these fish to draw them closer for photography, and they have thus been conditioned to crowd in whenever they see a camera.

...fish surrounding swimmers in a mad whirl of silver...

A dinghy trip along the shoreline in late afternoon yields an amusing sight among the rock cliffs. A mother goat and kid have grazed too near the nest of a pair of gulls, and the gulls are squawking with outrage. One of the irate gulls swoops at the kid, which jumps back a pace or two in surprise, then realizes that it has the size advantage and leaps toward the bird, head lowered as if ready to butt. The bird takes to the air and makes a half-hearted attempt at dive-bombing the pair. The goats continue on their way. The gulls settle down again, the danger past.

The goats continue on their way. The gulls settle down...

As we round a rocky point on our return to our anchorage in the Bight, we spot a lone brown booby perched on a rock. It shifts its feet and turns its beak in our direction, but apparently decides we are not a threat and holds its position as we dinghy past.

...we spot a lone brown booby perched on a rock...

The next day dawns partly cloudy. The weather here is constantly threatening. Clouds roll by, sometimes developing into towering thunderheads, but after a few minutes of rain, they roll on or dissipate. Nevertheless, the hatches must be closed to avoid getting the interior of the boat soaked. Hopefully, we set out buckets at the drip corners of our hardtop — nothing like rainwater for washing up. But we get, at most, an inch or two before the rain stops. In truth, these islands do not get much rainfall. At higher, cooler elevations, and on northern slopes, the vegetation is described as subtropical moist forest. Lower on the slopes, and on their southern and eastern sides, the forest becomes drier and more sparse. The trade winds and constant sunshine have created an arid landscape of cactus, century plants, and frangipani.

...cactus, century plants, and frantipani....

As we depart, we note that the building under construction next to Billy Bones Bar now has a finished plywood roof. What is the plan? Will it be a restaurant? Perhaps a gift shop, or a place that will rent kayaks and snorkel gear, or a store catering to the needs of cruisers, with water, garbage disposal, and ice? We have seen a motorboat with the clever name *Deliverance* doing a brisk business here in ice, water, and drinks as it putters from one anchored boat to another.

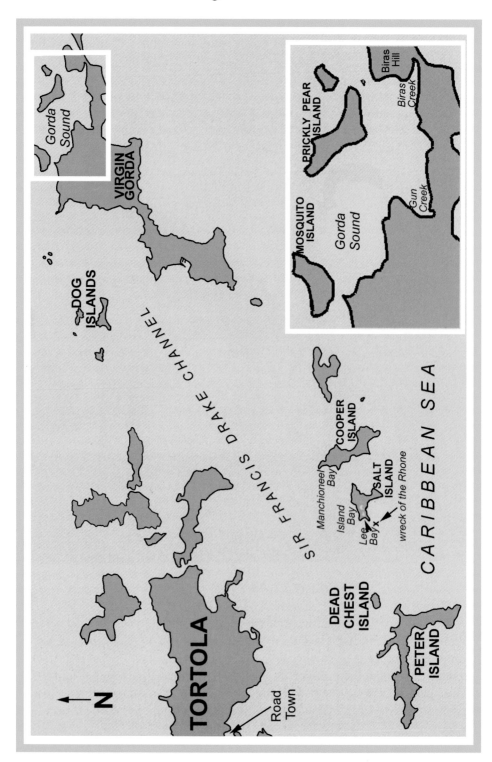

4: Salt Island to Virgin Gorda

We get a slow start in the morning, but eventually leave around 8 o'clock for the wreck of the *RMS Rhone* off Salt Island. The *Rhone*, a large passenger and cargo ship, sank over 100 years ago.   In those days before reliable weather forecasting, the ship's captain could not have known a hurricane was coming, though he must have observed that the barometric pressure was falling sharply, a sign of a serious storm on its way. As mighty hurricane winds began to blow he sailed off to ride out the storm at sea, but as the ship passed Salt Island, out of the protective lee of the land, savage winds hit the boat and dashed it into the rocks. Only three people of the hundreds aboard survived the grounding. The *Rhone's* remains lie in 30 to 80 feet of water, scattered in identifiable sections over a large area of seafloor.

We pass Pelican Island, a picturesque knob of rock, then Peter Island, and the exclusive Peter Island Yacht Harbour and Hotel complex. It does look posh,

...Pelican Island, a picturesque knob of rock...

with a beautiful beach. We also pass Dead Chest Island and wonder how pi-rates could possibly be stranded there, providing the basis for the well-known song ("Fifteen men on a dead man's chest"), since it is so close to Peter Island. Any pirate who could swim, or had sense enough to cobble together a raft out of driftwood, could easily cross the water to Peter Island, where he would find food and water.

We pull up to a red mooring in Lee Bay on Salt Island. This mooring is a non-diving day-use only mooring that does not require a permit. Dive boats are tied up to many of the diving moorings a hundred feet away. We dinghy the distance to the dinghy mooring, and find ourselves almost directly over the *Rhone*. Divers are spread out over the wreck and the surrounding reef, and we see few in the water. We gaze at a huge propellers, still recognizable all these years after the sinking.

...to look at the salt pond...

Later we dinghy to the beach off Island Bay, one bay over, to look at the salt pond. We steer the dinghy to the beach through breaking waves. There is coral, so we pick our way carefully. We land the dinghy and walk a short dis-tance over the beach and past uninhabited buildings at the north end of the beach. We see several more empty buildings at the other end of the beach, nestled among coconut palms. The salt pond, described in guidebooks as a working salt pond, where people come to collect salt to sell, does indeed have icy-looking lumps of salt encrusting the rocks around its edges.

...icy-looking lumps of salt...

We leave our mooring and head east to Manchioneel Bay on Cooper Island, just a couple of miles away. The anchorage is full of boats, all very close together and close to the land. Our depth-meter shows that the water is deep right up to the boats. We motor around awhile, looking for water less than 30 feet deep where we can put our anchor down, water shallow enough to dive to check the anchor if necessary, but no luck. We see nothing under 50 feet and we notice a prominent swell that will give us problems sleeping unless we are dead tired. We move on, looking for a better place.

We decide to sail all the way up to Gorda Sound at the northeast end of Virgin Gorda, about 15 miles away. This will be the longest sail we have had since arriving in the Virgin Islands, a clear demonstration of how close these islands are to each other.

We tack out west of the Dog Islands...

Since the wind is out of the east, we must motor or tack to reach Gorda Sound. We decide to sail without the motor, tacking back and forth across the Sir Francis Drake Channel, then sail into Gorda Sound through the north entrance between Colquhoun Reef and Cactus Reef. The wind is strong, 20 to 25 knots, and the seas are around 5 or 6 feet. Waves continually break over the top of the boat, so we close it up to keep it dry inside. We tack out west of the Dog Islands, and approach Virgin Gorda from the northwest.

We arrive at the north entrance at 5:30, about an hour before sunset. Though winds are gusting to 20 knots, the water in Gorda Sound is so protected that there is hardly a ripple on its surface. We continue to sail, right into the Sound and most of the way to the west side of Biras Hill. We lower our sails finally, and motor around, looking for a good place to anchor. Almost all of the boats here are on moorings. A few boats at the outer edges of the pack are anchored in 40 to 50 feet of water. We find a spot near the entrance of Biras Creek (it is actually a v-shaped cove, with no creek in sight or on our chart), and anchor a comfortable distance from other boats in 40 feet of water. The anchorage will be a quiet one, except for boat wakes. When Biras Creek's little ferry, *Helga*, comes by, it creates an enormous wake that sets us, and all the boats around us, rocking.

As we have drinks with cheese snacks, a laughing gull flies down to join us. He settles on the top of our dinghy outboard and begs for handouts. We toss him

Blooming flamboyant trees provide dappled shade...

a few, offering snide warnings about his little birdy arteries and his digestion, but he snatches each unhealthful orange tidbit out of the water and begs for more. Finally, either tired of us or gorged with cheese snacks, he departs. We turn out attention to the pelicans and laughing gulls clustering nearby. Their relationship is based on the gulls' desire to share what the pelicans catch. It goes like this: A pelican dives, capturing a fish or two or three in his bill, and bobs back up like a cork. At that instant, gull alights on the pelican's back, or sometimes, more precariously, on his head. The idea is to snap up any food the pelican drops. In these waters, every pelican seems to have his own laughing gull. What a nuisance!

In the morning we dinghy to the north side of Prickly Pear Island, a BVI park, and land at a long, lovely beach on the seaward side of the island. We spend an hour or so exploring the beach, where we pick up some pretty bottles for our son's collection. We find a vodka bottle covered with raised Cyrillic letters in clear glass. The glass of another bottle is decorated with stylized flowers and vines. We see many goats back in the trees. They wander away calmly at our approach. Clearly, they are used to people, and they want to avoid us.

We land our dinghy at the dinghy dock at the Bitter End Resort and have lunch at the English Pub. The Cuban sandwiches and draft John Smith beers are excellent. The setting is magical. Blooming flamboyant trees (known as royal poincianas back home) provide dappled shade for our *al fresco* meal on the Pub's terrace. Hummingbirds dart among the clusters of orange flowers overhead.

We explore the resort, noting a covered shelter with many benches where a big-screen TV is constantly turned on, providing entertainment for those starved for news of the busy world they left behind.

Helga comes to the resort dock, setting all the boats moored there trembling and rocking. The pilot ties the ferry up, walks to the Pub, and returns shortly with a white plastic-foam take-out box – *ah, lunch!* We make a guess: he's bought the one-quarter barbecued chicken for $4.50.

We leave Bitter End Resort and head out on a clockwise dinghy tour of Gorda Sound. We stop at the first bit of semi-sandy beach and discover goatskins draped over tree limbs. Somebody is making use of the feral goats here. We wonder what the goatskins will be used for. We continue close to shore down to the notch of Gun Creek, where the mystery of where *Helga* has been collecting its passengers is solved. Here is *Helga* again, her skipper having presumably consumed his lunch on the way to Gun Creek, and here are cars and tourist busses parked up and down the road. As we watch, a tourist bus drops off a handful of people and they board the little ferry. By and by, it leaves, trailing its fearsome wake.

From the water, the Gun Creek settlement is unappealing. Dead and dying boats litter the beach. We look up at tiny cottages perched on the hillside, some painted in bright colors and surrounded by well-tended gardens, bougainvilleas, and palms, others falling apart and deserted, overgrown. Cyril's Beach Bar, a turquoise concrete-block structure a little removed from Gun Creek, blasts out music as we pass.

...an upscale resort ...

We motor by an upscale resort complex with the stunningly unattractive name "Pusser's." All the buildings have red roofs. We soon arrive at the pass between Mosquito Island and Virgin Gorda. The water is open to the sea, and much rougher, almost too rough for our little dinghy. We stop to explore a small sandy beach on the Virgin Gorda side of the pass. There are heaps of rocks here, water-smoothed and rounded. Mollusks cling and climb over them. We identify large snail-shaped black-and-white turban shells.

...a small sandy beach on the Virgin Gorda side of the pass...

We reboard our dinghy, heading toward Mosquito Island. This little island is off-limits to the likes of us (unless we want to spend some money at its exclusive restaurant). We pass it by, happy to gaze upon the diners who are gazing out at us. We pass Prickly Pear Island and are soon back where we started, but extremely pleased with ourselves, for haven't we seen everything there is to see in Gorda Sound?

...Prickly Pear Island...

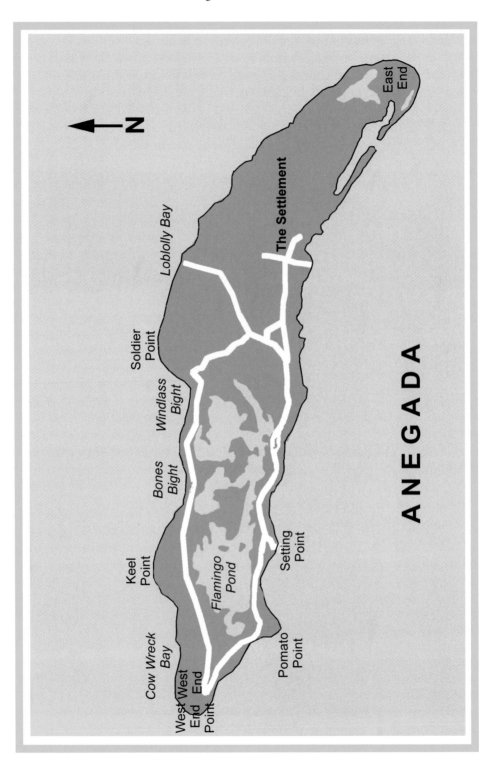

5: Anegada

Morning, and a decision point. We are eager to visit Anegada, an island north of Virgin Gorda, off by itself 13 miles away and a world apart. The island is famous for its beautiful, wild, unspoiled beaches and gorgeous reefs. Virgin Gorda is closest to Anegada, and the obvious point of departure for us, but the question is timing. Should we go now? We listen to BVI radio 780 AM at 8:05 for the marine forecast. A tropical wave has come through, bringing rain. Over the next few days the winds will freshen, reaching 20 to 25 knots by tomorrow. We must leave now or wait for quieter weather that might be coming along five days from now.

We sail easily and quickly, with 15 to 20 knots of wind from the east and 2- to 4-foot seas. We single-reef the main, but find we don't need it. We average over 6 knots, and make the passage in about 2 hours. We put down the sails as we reach the red and green buoys marking the entrance to the anchorage off Setting Point.

...the anchorage off Setting Point.

We motor past Setting Point and find a spot to anchor at the west end of the anchorage, near Pomato Point, in 6 feet of water. The bottom is sand and grass, and appears to be good holding, but in this shallow water, the first we've seen in the Virgins, we put out about 60 feet of anchor rode just to be sure.

...a procession of Moorings charter boats...

We sit back in our new anchorage and watch a procession of Moorings charter boats follow us in, 17 boats in all. All but one anchors or moors on the east side of the anchorage, close to Setting Point. One motors back toward us, then moves across our bow to a point a little closer to land. He is instantly aground, running his engines in a desperate attempt to escape, churning up grass and sand. He gives that up and gets into his dinghy with his anchor, drops the anchor, snorkels to look for deeper water. We know he has the cell phone issued to all Moorings charter boat customers — will he use it to get help? The answer is yes. Here comes a small blue motorboat manned by an Anegadan.

The rescuer pushes his boat's bow against the sailboat's bow, shoving the bow around until the sailboat is pointed toward deeper water. Next he goes down to the stern of the sailboat and plants the boat's bow against the sailboat's stern, giving it a push from the rear. The charterer helps by engaging the sailboat motor. Soon the sailboat is free of the shallows. Clouds of sand fill the water all around the sailboat. Free at last, the unstuck captain motors off to join the other charter sailboats in the deeper water closer to Setting Point. He has learned his lesson, and it is one that is not lost on others that are now arriving in groups of two and three boats at a time, dropping their sails as they slip between the entrance buoys. We remain in isolation in our little anchorage until another catamaran arrives. No other boats risk travel through these shallows, though, and we are pleased with our choice. It may be shallow, and far from the bright lights of the Anegada Reef Hotel and its convenient dinghy dock, but it is — almost — all ours.

We are eager to see the beaches, so we depart in our dinghy after lunch, travel-ing west along the shore. Minutes into our trip we come upon a lone rock barely submerged between us and Pomato Point. We nearly hit it. The water in this bay is not particularly clear, probably due to the strong wind and waves stirring up the shallow waters. Though the sun is directly overhead, the choppy waves make it hard to see submerged hazards. A line of rocks extends 50 feet or so from Pomato Point: these we easily avoid as we surf around the point in a 20-knot tailwind.

We land on the west side of Pomato Point and begin to explore the island. We find that, as mentioned in the guidebooks, there are orchids everywhere in the island interior just a few steps beyond the beach. Some are wiry-leaved yellow clumps of terrestrial plants with many foot-tall flower heads bearing white and pink flowers. Others are cliff orchids, plants that grow in the lower branches of the scrubby island trees. These have gray-green leaves and amazing four- to seven-foot-tall stems tipped with many tiny, complicated blooms of pink and chartreuse that bob gently in the breeze. We take a few pictures, difficult on a windy, cloudy day like today. The orchids won't stand still, and their colors are muted in the shade from passing clouds. For anyone who believes

...Some are wiry-leaved terrestrial plants..Others are cliff orchids...

the orchid is a delicate, hothouse flower, requiring bright, cool, moist conditions, here is proof of its hardiness. These plants are living and flourishing in the most difficult of environments, lashed by constant wind and salt spray, baking under a hot sun.

We walk the beach for a while, then head back in the dinghy to West End. We pass two sailboats anchored in the bay west of Pomato Point. They represent either a lot of courage or substantial local knowledge. Here the water is shallow and filled with coral heads and the entrance to the bay is unmarked. If we were to try this anchorage, we would have to arrive during a period of calm water, and we would be extremely cautious coming in, one of us up front

We walk the beach for a while...

calling out visible hazards and one steering with a careful eye on the depth-meter.

Tiny rental cottages on the beach near Pomato Point have covered porches looking out on the sea and the louvered windows so common in this area, with no sign of air conditioners anywhere around them. Indeed, the sea breeze remains fairly steady and only the few hours in the middle of the day could be described as hot, even now, in late May. Like all the homes on this island, the cottages are fenced. Here, as everywhere in the Virgins, feral donkeys, goats, and cattle wander freely and if you don't want to share your space with them, you have to fence your yard.

...the exact place that comes to mind when one imagines a tropical paradise...

We stop in quiet water just west of West End Point and walk the beach. It is empty of people and houses. Here is the exact place that comes to mind when one imagines a tropical paradise: a beautiful, isolated white sand beach, a turquoise sea, cool breezes, clear skies. We walk for a couple of miles and see nobody else.

Back in the dinghy we head home for drinks. We count 26 boats in the harbor! This place is crowded, but except for the one catamaran that anchored nearby before we left, the boats are far away, and they are behind us out of sight when we sit in the back of the boat looking out. Beyond our stern we see only sky, beach, and water. With our sunset gin-and-tonics we toast vistas such as this one all over the world, being enjoyed at this very moment by fortunate people like us.

In the morning we load the dinghy with lunch and plenty of soft drinks and water with the intention of exploring the island's beaches. We are soon at West End. We continue on past Cow Wreck Bay, where we see a restaurant/beach bar. We have noticed that the few buildings on the beach all seem to have a commercial purpose, though they are not marked as such as viewed from the beach. The oversized signs we know from Florida beaches are absent here. The owners of these establishments obviously understand that a name has no cachet for their customers, mostly cruisers, and that copious signage does nothing but spoil the view, and we think *good on them*.

After Cow Wreck Bay on the northwest end of the island our dinghy route becomes increasingly perilous. We proceed very carefully around the rocks and reefs. A continuous reef on the north side lies but a few hundred feet off the land and is easily identified by the breaking surf. We travel between that reef and the beach through a maze of underwater hazards. There are rocks and parts of reef often visible above water, and many rocks and reefs just below the surface. We look for white sandy areas, or areas that are covered with grasses, to motor over.

Eventually we work our way through Bones Bight and Windlass Bight, and beach our dinghy at Soldier Point, about half way down the north side of the island. After a short walk we put up a tarp between the dinghy and two driftwood poles we find on the beach. We eat our lunch in the shade, and talk through the heat of the day.

At 2:30 we take to the water in snorkel gear. We rediscover the hazards we avoided in the morning's dinghy ride, this time from underwater. Isolated rocks rise from the sandy floor, covered with corals and sponges and anemones, tiny bright reef fish darting in and out of their crevices and caves. Here a tall branching coral formation the color of sand rises right to the surface of the water. There a shelf of rock, plastered with purple sponges and cream-colored corals, splits the sandy floor. We are astounded at the rock shelves, the

...corals and sponges...bright reef fish...

coral heads — how did we make it through this maze in the dinghy? But we also see the grass-bottomed arroyos and the broad sandy plains, many nearer the beach, that we followed to this place.

The trip back to *Top Cat* later in the afternoon is not easy. For part of the trip we are traveling into the sun — the dark patches that mark reef and grassy shallows are hard to see before they are too close to avoid. We slide into some grassy banks and once we hit a rock that stops our engine. We are moving slowly, however, and sustain no damage to our prop. On our arrival at our boat, we count 31 boats in the harbor. They are still coming. We thought we would be alone on Anegada, because we read that many charter companies make the island off-limits to their customers. Now that we are here, we see how foolish it would be to prohibit a trip to Anegada. The island is a jewel, a precious little piece of Virgin Island paradise!

The next day we rent a car at the Anegada Reef Hotel to explore the island by land. We leave *Catnap* tied at the dinghy dock and carry our gear — cameras, drinks, snorkel gear — to our car.

...we rent a car at the Anagada Reef Hotel...

The car comes with instructions of several kinds. We must drive on the left-hand side of the road, limiting our speed to 30 miles an hour. We must stay on the main roads, as indicated by solid lines on our map. If we get stuck, we must push on the frame of the car, not the panels. We must not to drive on the beach. We must leave the key in the ignition when we leave the car, a rule that sounds peculiar (what, they *want* somebody to steal it?) until we realize that a car simply could not be stolen here, or if stolen, could never be used. This island is too small for such a crime to go unpunished. Somebody would spot the stolen vehicle, probably within hours, and the jig would be up. Clearly, the larger danger to these cars is that a driver will take the key along on a snorkeling or beachcombing adventure and lose it.

The one instruction we do not find in our car or written materials is that the car can only be started through the use of a choke. We are flummoxed for a while, trying and trying to start it, until a helpful hotel worker comes by, leans in, and shows us what to do.

The trip overland is no less a hazardous journey than the trip by dinghy. The main roads are mostly sand and rock, and are very bumpy. The car is a Suzuki with 4-speed manual shift on the floor without air conditioning or radio, a stripped-down model built for action. This car is a survivor. Its condition testifies to long use under these wild island conditions.

We stop along the road to get a picture of a nearby salt pond. A pair of donkeys graze along the shores. They spot us and trot quickly into the brush. From this vantage point they spy on us, apparently imagining they are hidden from view, but we can see their tall ears poking up above the shrubbery.

A pair of donkeys graze along the shores.

We drive off the road to visit a salt pond. Here the land is crisscrossed with tracks testifying to considerable traffic, so we feel sure this is a safe route to

...probably the only place on the island without beaches.

follow. The banks of the pond are very broad. We drive to a point about 50 feet from the water, and all seems well as we climb out of the car. We walk around a bit, and take a picture or two, but when we turn back to the car, *catastrophe!* The car has taken advantage of our absence to settle in. We get in and start the car, hoping for the best, but it has sunk about 4 inches into the mud, and the wheels spin as the engine roars. We push (on the frame, not the doors or panels). We rock the car back and forth. We can't seem to climb out of our hole. However, the rocking digs four short trenches under the wheels, and this gives us an idea. We pave these trenches with flat rocks we find scattered among the brush a short and slippery walk from the car. We back out over our rocky ramps. We are free! We decide to follow more carefully the direction to stick to the main roads, and in any case to avoid the banks of salt ponds.

We head east to The Settlement, the only town on the island. As we near the town the dirt road becomes concrete, raised a few inches off the surrounding ground. It gives the odd effect of driving on a narrow concrete ramp. The town has a scattering of buildings, a very pretty church, a school, a weedy but exceptionally nice basketball court where a goat grazes, and many small, neatly shuttered houses with corrugated metal roofs, each with its own little plot of land carefully fenced all around. The town, we are surprised to see, has not been built on the water, but is about a half-mile back from it. The water's edge just south of the town is a stretch of mangrove mudflats, probably the only

...islands made of conchs...

place on the island without beaches. From the town dock we can see islands made of heaps of conchs, attesting to the popularity of that shellfish as food.

We stop at Dotsy's, a bakery with a covered dining area out front so the delectables purchased in the bakery can be consumed on the spot. We order coffee and banana bread. A jaunty little bananaquit flits in and out of the dining area, occasionally stopping to grasp the screen under the door louvers and peer in. He must be familiar with Dotsy's delights. Perhaps she feeds him crumbs to keep him coming around; we hope so. Dotsy's bread is delicious, with flavors of nutmeg and cinnamon, and a fine, velvety texture, and the coffee is good and hot, in big white mugs placed on pretty china saucers. We buy a loaf of coconut bread that looks like a small brown pie to take with us.

We head north to Loblolly Bay. We are amazed at the piles of cow dung on both sides of the road. Here, we can see, cattle are a major factor in the environment. We wonder what they find to eat on the scrub- and cactus-covered island, and whether they are slaughtered or made use of in any way by the

Anegadans or left to roam and multiply like sacred cows in India. We turn in at the town dump and take a picture of three of them calmly munching cardboard. Returning to the road, we pass the new government building, clearly the handsomest and sturdiest building on this island. We pass the school, where five or six junior-high-age children in uniforms play ball in the driveway. Then the concrete pavement ends – we look up and ahead — can this be a road? — And we jounce uphill over the bumpiest dirt and rock track imaginable. We wouldn't drive our own car on this road. It wouldn't survive the shaking. The road, though rough, provides a view of the wild, beautiful interior of the island, covered with cactus plants of various kinds. In places, it is bordered by low masonry walls constructed of coral rock. We have read that these walls were built by the Danes hundreds of years ago.

The island is 9 miles long and a few miles wide. It doesn't take long to arrive on the north side. We stop at Flash of Beauty Restaurant and Bar at Loblolly

...Flash of Beauty Restaurant and Bar...

Bay where a curving line of queen conchs, set up on their larger ends, delineates the parking area. There are three such eateries on the bay, separated by respectful distances. A reef a few hundred feet off the beach provides quiet water for swimming and snorkeling. We see breaking surf everywhere offshore. The bay itself is dappled dark green, black, and brown with reefs and rocks, separated here and there by patches of sandy bottom. A sign warns against poaching and specifies what may not be taken — there are conchs, lobsters, and crabs here, it seems.

We see breaking surf everywhere offshore.

We walk the beach and return to have lunch at the open-air restaurant. The cook-waitress-bartender, the only person here, rises from her books. She laughs when we comment on her studies ("back to school at a ripe old age") and fetches a couple of beers and a menu for us. We have a hamburger and a fish sandwich, identified as trunkfish by our waitress, who shows us a card of fish pictures so we will know what we are getting. Trunkfish is a reef fish that we often see as we snorkel here and elsewhere. It is a bony little creature shaped like a valise, flat on the bottom and curved on top. Propelled by miniature fins, it seems poorly balanced, as if a touch will turn it over on its side or send it tumbling through the water totally out of control. We have never thought of the trunkfish as a promising food fish. But the trunkfish sandwich is good and goes very well with the beer. (We order another beer, to share.) We look out at the spectacular bay from the shade of the restaurant, the breeze wafting through, as we devour our lunch.

Three Germans walk in as we are eating and seat themselves at the bar, where they order drinks. They say they took a taxi to the beach and were let off at one of the other restaurant bars on the bay. They are from the Frankfurt area, on a three-week vacation in the BVI. They speak excellent English to us, but return to their conversation in German when their drinks arrive.

After lunch we snorkel the bay. Coral heads and reefs rise from the sand bottom to near the surface. In many places the coral formations are in 6 to 8 feet of water on a floor of very white sand. Near the shore, in shallow water, a strong enough current runs to make snorkeling perilous. The corals reach upward; some of their tops are out of the water today. The narrow channels between the rocks and coral heads make for difficult maneuvering. The wind or current could easily push a snorkeler into sharp coral or rock. Underwater arches and caves offer complex formations in tight quarters. We snorkel for some time and manage not to hurt ourselves — or the corals.

Back in the car we complete our trip around the island. We head back to The Settlement, then west. We stop at the bridge to look for 22 flamingos, imported from Bermuda and plunked down in Anegada's Flamingo Bay to give the name a little authenticity. They inhabit one spot on the island several miles from the nearest road. We see them (or perhaps just think we see them) as pinkish shoreline specks in the far distance. Looking south off the bridge, in a trickle of tidal flow over a sandy plain, we see jolly brown pelicans. They are better than some specks on the distant shoreline and we take some pictures.

...jolly brown pelicans...

We head west past the hotel and our anchorage to West End, then past Cow Wreck Bay to Bones Bight. We stop along the way to take more pictures of orchids. Orchids are everywhere! Our Anegada information brochure says that orchids here bloom for most of the year starting in February or March.

Orchids are everywhere!

We walk around a little on the beach at Bones Bight, remembering it from when we passed it in the dinghy. Back in our transport, we continue along the road passing frangipani trees dotted with white pinwheel blooms, century plants with 10-foot-tall stalks of golden blooms, tall slender cacti with crowded upright stems like the pipes of a church organ. We pass an enormous expanse of salt pond below us and to our right.

The main road on the north side of the island is sand as fluffy as snowdrifts, but we manage not to get stuck. Eventually we complete our trip and arrive back at the hotel. We have traveled perhaps a total of 25 miles at an average speed of less than 10 m.p.h.. Our top speed was 28 m.p.h., over a hard-packed sand road. It's been a full day's adventure. We turn in the car, pleased that we have no damage to report despite our early problems with mud.

We eye the anchorage in surprise.   — Only a handful of boats remain.

As we head for the dock, we pass three big metal barbecue drums that have been filled with wood . Fires blaze in preparation for the hotel restaurant's nightly feast. Halfway along the dock three men stand amid dozens of enormous live lobsters. One of them flips the lobsters up on the dock and slits them open. Somebody will have lobster for supper tonight, but not us. We dinghy back to the boat, enjoy our gin-and-tonics, and eat a supper from cans with the delicious amendment of coconut bread from Dotsy's.

A new day dawns, and not such a fine one. Gray skies all around, drizzle intermixed with outright rain. We break out the water collectors. The sky is giving back to us what we lost in perspiration yesterday.

Another tropical wave has come through. These are low pressure areas that move from east to west through the Caribbean basin frequently in the summer, about as often as fronts move from the west to the east over North America in the winter. We are at the end of May, very early in the season for tropical waves, so we don't expect strong ones. The waves bring rain, and increased winds as well. Now they spend themselves and peter out; later on in the summer and into early fall, some of these waves will develop into tropical depressions, then tropical storms, and a few will turn into hurricanes.

We use up the morning reading, writing, and doing boat chores. In the afternoon the rains subside enough for a dinghy trip. We head south and west, and see a big upside-down boat on a sand bank off the west end. The boat has a flat bottom. Farther on we see a group of kids on the beach near tents, and off the beach an old sailboat anchored. Perhaps they are a youth group on a camping trip. We pass Ruffin Point and West End Point, and drop our dinghy anchor offshore in a patch of white sand near one of the reef areas.

...a big upside-down boat on a sand bank...

As we head west, we are out of the direct path of the east wind for the first time. The wind and waves stir up the coral sand bottom, making the water murky. But here, off the west end of the island, the water is clear. We snorkel past a wreck that is completely integrated into the reef. Pieces of boat and patches of coral are intertwined, as if they had grown together. Around the reef is turtlegrass and cleared sandy areas in water from 5 to 7 feet deep. We take care not to get blown into the reef in the 15-knot winds.

We return to *Top Cat* to find that we have been joined in our shallow anchorage by two new boats. One, a large catamaran, has many passengers, including several children. Everyone is in the water swimming and snorkeling around the boat. The couple in the monohull directly in front of us return in their dinghy; the gentleman doffs his clothing and comes out on deck wearing his birthday suit. Many people see cruising in the Virgins as an opportunity to walk around naked. It's certainly true that the best way to save precious freshwater stores while washing up is to scrub up and rinse in the ocean, and then again sparingly in fresh water. Many remain in their swimming suits for these ablutions; some do not. Many also just sit naked on the back steps of their boats to use the freshwater showers installed at that location.

The night brings a noisy rainstorm. We are forced to close the boat up against the torrents. We can't sleep because of the howling wind and slapping waves, but we are glad the boat is getting a rinsing and our water-catching containers are out under the drip corners of the hardtop, collecting rainwater.

In the morning the weather appears to be improving. We are many gallons of water ahead. On the other hand, we are out of bread, and since our traditional lunch is sandwiches on the go, we must have bread. We dinghy over to Pam's Kitchen at the Neptune's Treasure resort complex to buy some bread. Pam displays a weather map printed out from the Internet. The map and forecast indicates better weather is indeed on its way.

We load the dinghy with drinks and lunch, two chairs, and our trusty plastic K-Mart tarpaulin. We head west around the island. We plan to set up a day camp near Keel Point. We stay close to the beach for the trip, avoiding thin water above reefs, heads, and grassy flats. Many hazards lie along our path. The first is a submerged rock between our boat and Pomato Point, about two thirds of the way to the point. Next, a line of coral reef extends outward from Pomato Point. The reef here is half above water at the point, and the sea from the east always provides large swells and individual peaking waves as we round the point wide to clear the rocks. At the next point we hug the shore to avoid a long stretch of rocks and reef that stretch out from the point. We sneak through a narrow passage between the rocks and shoreline. We continue to hug the shore, skirting the dark coral patches, for the remainder of our trip. Having made this trip six times now, we are experts.

We secure our tarp between two dead trees, the broken stump of a third, and our dinghy, pulled well up the beach. Though aflap, it provides shelter from the sun and any rainshowers that might come along. We immediately spot two large fish, perhaps tarpon, patrolling just offshore. We take a long walk and when we return to our shelter we are accompanied most of the way in the water by a small shark.

We are accompanied...by a small shark.

We secure our tarp between two dead trees...

Now it's time to return to *Top Cat* and get dressed for the lobster supper we are treating ourselves to at the Anagada Reef Hotel. We are a few minutes late, but not to worry — our food is still on the grill. We take a closer look at the cookers, 50-gallon steel drums cut in half lengthwise. One half holds the coals, the other becomes a cover when the cooker is not in use. The cook starts the process early in the evening by burning pieces of wood in the cookers, with the fires visible from any sailboat in the harbor. Tonight only one cooker is in use, tended by a man wielding a long-handled fork. The grill is covered with rows of foil-wrapped split lobsters, steaks, and thick filets of fish.

The servers are pretty young ladies dressed in white shirts and long, black-and-white print skirts. One of them shows us to our places at a wooden picnic table. We order a bottle of 1996 California chardonnay on the theory that imported wines are the best ones; the lobster arrives with the wine and with side dishes of potatoes, carrots, corn on the cob, and a small pitcher of melted butter. We each have a whole, huge lobstertail. We are astonished to discover that we are able to eat every last morsel of our lobstertails. Our server brings dessert, luscious chocolate cream pie, heavy on the chocolate. We dinghy back to the boat in the dark, happily filled with delicious food and $102 poorer.

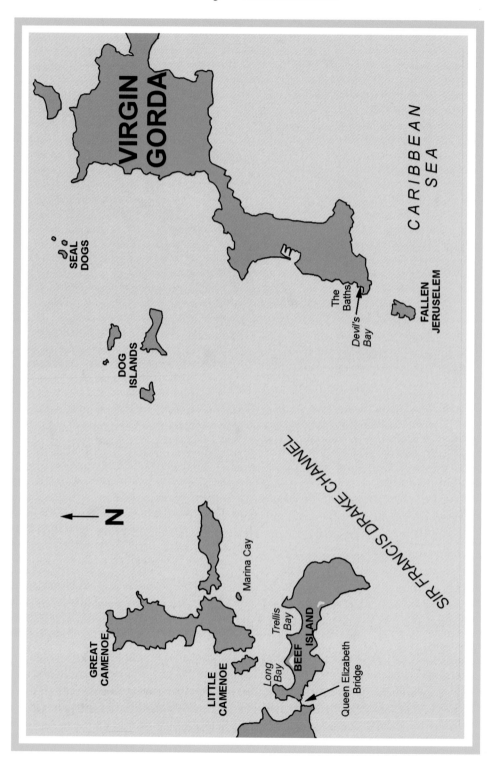

6: The Baths to Trellis Bay

Morning. It's time to go. We take up the anchor at 7 o'clock, sad that we're leaving this beautiful spot but eager for new adventures and new vistas. The trip back to Virgin Gorda is bumpy, with winds upward of 25 knots and seas of 3 to 5 feet, but it is fast, and we make good time. We sail with a single reef and in under two hours we are nearing Virgin Gorda.

We pass Spanish Town and then we reach our destination, The Baths, near the southern tip of Virgin Gorda. We quickly tie up on a day-use-only mooring. It is late morning, so we will have many hours here. Anchoring is not a good idea, as the bottom is very rocky, true of much of the west side of Virgin Gorda, and is poor holding ground.

...the bottom is very rocky...and poor holding ground...

The Baths consists of hundreds of huge granite boulders jumbled atop each other for about a half mile along the shoreline. The spaces between these boulders are fantastic caves and crevices, some with sand floors, others holding quiet pools of seawater — hence the name, The Baths.

We dinghy to the beach nearest The Baths and explore on foot. The BVI park service has developed a trail between The Baths and Devil's Bay that utilizes ropes and ladders to help the hiker over steep slopes and wooden bridges for crossing gaps between adjacent boulders. Some of the watersmoothed granite boulders are more than 50 feet across.

...a trail utilizes ladders...

Part of the trail requires a wade through shallow water and we are glad we wore our water shoes. Many hikers we meet along the way are barefooted. The trail is marked with arrows dabbed in concrete on the granite boulders.

Part of the trail requires a wade through shallow water...

Off the main trail we detour along paths that dead-end in lovely cul-de-sacs, some with cascades of roots from trees growing above, some with window-like openings above that let a single shaft of light penetrate the cool darkness, some that open out onto lovely views of the rocks and the blue see beyond them. The beautiful rooms of The Baths are decorated by nature and shaped by the powerful forces of weather and the sea, truly one of the natural wonders of the world. It is easy to understand their popularity.

...some that open out onto lovely views...

...The Baths...

We finally emerge from the darkness of The Baths at a pretty beach at Devil's
Bay. Time for a hike, since there is a trail here. We continue upward on a path
toward the parking lot.

...a pretty beach at Devil's Bay...

It winds through the brush and boulders of a hilly terrain. Large lizards with
electric blue stripes in their tails scurry out of our way; we glance back over
our shoulders now and then at the sparkling water of Drake's Passage below.
We are on a tropical island, and yet the jumble of boulders and sparse vegetation bring Colorado to mind.

...the jumble of boulders and sparse vegetation bring Colorado to mind.

We continue on up the trail and eventually arrive at the parking lot, a distance of 600 yards from The Baths. Here the trail branches off to the right, wending its way down to a small beach on the water and presents an excellent view of Fallen Jerusalem, the nearest island to the south. Another trail goes out to a

...an excellent view of Fallen Jeruselem...

boulder field, and gives us an opportunity to climb the rocks for even better views. At the parking lot we can see much of Virgin Gorda stretching to the north of us. From here we can head south by climbing, but the trail is covered with thorny underbrush. We barge ahead anyway, and find a few tall boulders to climb on that provide views of the islands and of luxurious homes to the north.

...even better views.

In the afternoon we snorkel the area from The Baths to Devil's Bay. The water is clear, with visibility over 100 feet. As on the surface, big boulders dominate the scenery, but these are decorated with corals and surrounded by brightly hued reef fish — and lots of snorkelers. The water is 20 or more feet deep, with boulders reaching up from the sandy sea floor to near or above the water's surface. We enter one area between large boulders and find ourselves trapped within a boulder field. We retreat and continue south to Devil's Bay. The underwater corals become more interesting as we approach Devil's Bay.

...boulders...decorated with corals and surrounded by...reef fish...

Late in the afternoon we leave The Baths and cross the sound under sail. We are heading to Trellis Bay at Beef Island, and what we hope will be a quiet anchorage. The trip is downwind, and easy, but as we approach the Trellis Bay area we note big swells from the east, and lots of white-capped waves. It will be difficult to leave here against a strong east wind.

We round south into Trellis Bay past two small rocks marked with a buoy, and anchor near the northern end at about 6 o'clock. Our anchorage lies between and behind a large catamaran from South Africa and an old wooden ketch whose deck is covered with plants. We look around. This anchorage shelters many boats, and nearly all of them on fee-for-use moorings. We are (misery!) not far from Tortola's international airport, which means that ferries, all with amazing wakes, go and come fairly continuously.

...Trellis Bay...

Not long after we settle down with our drinks on the back of the boat, a dinghy approaches piloted by a young blond woman in a bathing suit. She adroitly attaches her dinghy to our lifeline. She opens a case containing bright enamel and cast resin pins, barrettes, and pendants, and proceeds with her sales pitch. She explains that she lives on a boat here in Trellis Bay — the one with the black mast — with her young son and husband. She has lived in the Virgins for 14 years, but she is originally from Montreal. Her strange accent may indeed be French, but it sounds to us more like Valley Girl. The jewelry she is selling, she says, she makes. We look over her merchandise and choose a key ring, at $10 the cheapest item in her box. Satisfied that she has made at least one sale, she moves on to the next new boat.

Another morning, and a beautiful day. A few puffy clouds rim the horizon. The wind blows gently. Today we will do some chores and explore. We dinghy off to do our laundry at Marina Cay, a tiny island across the water, and to snorkel in the rocks around it.

Marina Cay has a beautiful anchorage, certainly one of the nicest in the British Virgins. The long reef to the east has produced a very clean white sandy bottom in the anchorage, inviting the snorkeler. The water becomes increasingly shallow up to the place where breaking waves meet the bones of an old reef in inches of water. The best snorkeling is at the edges of the reef in the north or south. The area just northeast of the cay has many more corals. We anchor our dinghy in a sandy patch in 8 feet of water directly north of the cay and snorkel east to the edge of the reef. The water is clear; many coral heads dot the white sandy bottom. Though the reef is sparse here, it provides fine snorkeling. No need to worry about being pushed into a coral or find oneself in a box canyon of reef walls that suddenly rise toward the surface, as in Anegada. We spot many parrotfish, several kinds of puffers, and large schools of tiny silver fish.

Marina Cay has a beautiful anchorage...

Between snorkeling forays, we wash and then dry our clothes, making trips back and forth to feed money into the machines. The laundry facilities are very convenient, though expensive, at $3 per machine. Showers are also available at $1, but we are quite satisfied with the primitive facilities on our boat, and pass up the chance at hot water and complete privacy. Pusser's has a store here, and a restaurant, and the fuel dock is very easy to tie up to in a big boat. After lunch we set out in our dinghy to reprovision our boat. We are awed by the prices, but must have mayonnaise, bread, sandwich meat, bananas, and veg. We add two ice-cold beers to our basket.

After a lunch of sandwiches, bananas, and beer, we dinghy over to Little Camanoe Island, about a mile to our northwest. The island is uninhabited. Two beaches lie side by side, separated by a boulder the size of a dump truck marking the tip of the island, a spot with the colorful name of Pull and Be Damn Point. The coral heads in the waters around the island look interesting from the dinghy, but they are too close to the surface and too close together for us to snorkel them in the wind and rough sea off the island today.

...Little Canenoe Island...

We hike up the gentle slope of the island on the northeast side and encounter a group of goats. All rush off in a hurry except one. We creep up on him and try to engage him in conversation. He instantly retreats. None of the goats in the Virgins like people. We walk carefully — small and very prickly cacti hide in the grass here. The views are good from every vantage point around the island. We look across to the south and see Long Bay. Its beach is obviously

All rush off in a hurry except one.

...the Queen Elizabeth Bridge...

popular, and is easily accessible off the road. We see fast motorboats with big outboards whizzing noisily in and out of the bay. To the north is Great Camanoe, another island with many houses on it. To the southeast we see Beef Island, a mountain that towers over all the other land masses.

We continue around the coast of Beef Island and see ahead of us the Queen Elizabeth Bridge, which crosses the Beef Island Channel and connects Beef Island to Tortola. We watch a big white truck loaded with Tortolans rumble across to Beef Island. Later we will see it parked opposite our anchorage at Trellis Bay, as the passengers enjoy the pretty boulder-strewn public beach there. A reef extends through the Beef Island Channel; the channel is marked with buoys, and follows the edge of the reef. We go under the bridge, and out into Sir Francis Drake Channel.

...crosses the Beef Island Channel and connects Beef Island to Tortola.

It is rough on this side of the channel, too rough for our little dinghy. We drift into the shallows and struggle to get ourselves back into water deep enough to put down our motor. Finally, we are on our way. We quickly return back under the bridge to calmer water.

On the way back to our anchorage we explore a tiny mangrove-rimmed cove. The water is clear and unrumpled. Boats are tied up to the mangroves. This is a safe place for a small boat, we think, and it has an interesting ecology. The clear unrumpled water provides us a view of underwater life.

Colorful sponges festoon the mangrove roots.We pass over sessile jellyfish like plump green doilies, pulsing gently. We see a feather duster and a bug-eyed orange squirrelfish. We see a two-inch fish with a much smaller fish in its jaws. It zigs and zags to escape pursuing fish that want to share its meal, and rushes around mangrove roots at top speed to avoid its pursuers. Then *gulp!* the captured fish is gone. Which fish has eaten it? It's impossible to say.

...a tiny mangrove-rimmed cove.

Colorful sponges...a feather duster...

The day is waning. Time for our sunset gin-and-tonics. Tonight we have ar-
ranged a treat for ourselves – dinner and a show at The Last Resort, a restaurant on a tiny island in the middle of Trellis Bay, about 200 yards from where
we are anchored. We have watched a donkey amble around the grounds of the
restaurant, nibbling at the vegetation, and on occasion disappear inside the
restaurant! What's up with that? We intend to find out.

We grab a flashlight and our pole-mounted dinghy light and dinghy over.
The dinghy dock is well-lit. We follow the lighted walkway to the restaurant.
At this end we can see the bar, and also about a half-dozen dogs lying about as
if they are exhausted from a hard day's work. We are escorted to our table;
drink orders are taken. We look around. The restaurant is decorated in Spanish colonial, with dark wood beams overhead, brightly painted papier maché
sculptures and straw figurines hanging on the wall, and big wrought-iron yel-
low-globed lights. A bookcase overflows with paperbacks, obviously a take-
one, leave-one swap-out library for cruisers. In front of us is the "bandstand"
— amps and a control panel in the front and a display of stringed instruments
on the wall behind. A white cat lounges on the equipment, occasionally rous-
ing itself to stretch and find somewhere new for serial napping.

To start the meal, we are given a pureed vegetable soup and slices of fine-
textured white bread. Very tasty. Next comes the salad, which we serve ourselves at the buffet, well-oiled greens and a mixture of beans. We ask for water
and an iced pitcherful is delivered to our table.

The buffet is ready. We line up to serve ourselves. We have our choice of
chicken, roast beef, or fish; dark, airy rolls that turn out to taste like popovers;
and a variety of vegetable and pasta dishes, all very good. At the end of the
meal comes dessert, our choice of cake and ice cream or strawberries and ice
cream. Suddenly, the donkey is among us, part of the decor, having stuck her
head through a hole near the buffet table. Her name, according to the decorative frieze around the hole, is Vanilla. The kitchen staff has brought carrot
peelings and bits of celery the guests may hand-feed her. There's the answer to
our question about the mysterious donkey.

Tony Snell, who normally performs nightly at The Last Resort, is on vacation,
and his replacement is Orville Griffiths, a singer/guitar player with an infec-
tious laugh. He apologizes for not being a funnyman like Tony, but sings a
song about eating chicken heads and tells some elevator jokes. When he pauses
between songs, he is urged by knowledgeable patrons to "blow the harmonica."

He finds the harmonica amidst the clutter of CDs on the bandstand and blows. A half-dozen dogs come rushing from all over, barking excitedly. Tails wagging, they face him and begin to howl. When he stops blowing, they stop howling almost instantly and walk away. It is very funny, and Orville blows the harmonica again and again, with precisely the same result. It is a real crowd-pleaser and the dogs never seem to tire of it.

After the show, we head home through the blackest of nights. The batteries of our dinghy light are fading and so are our flashlight batteries, but we locate *Top Cat* in the anchorage without much trouble. Exhausted from a day of snorkeling and hiking, we sleep well.

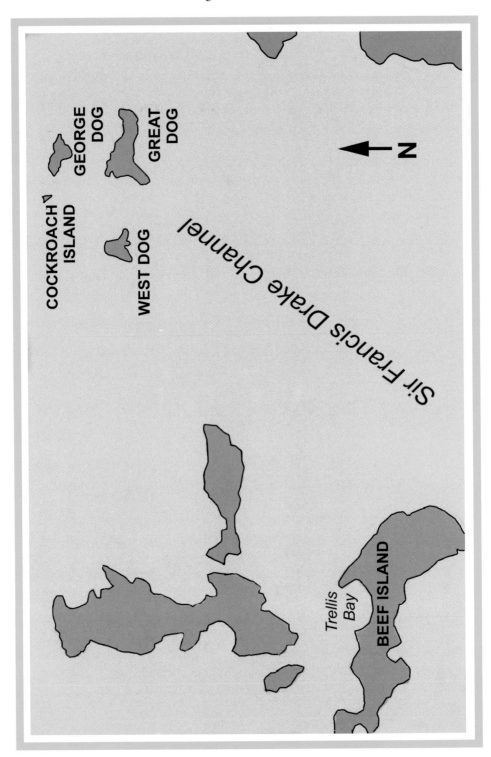

7: Going to the Dogs

We leave Trellis Bay in the morning for the Dog Islands a few miles away. They are famous for excellent diving and snorkeling. We pass Cockroach Island and sail between West Dog and Great Dog, headed for George Dog. The islands look grand in the morning light, with green slopes and rocks, but we see no goats. Perhaps this is one of the few places in the Virgins without goats!

...The islands look grand in the morning light ...

We arrive by 9 o'clock and pick up a dive mooring on the southwest end of George Dog. Another boat arrives at the same time and picks up the other mooring to our east. We start out using our floating air compressor with regulators attached. This rig allows us to dive to 30 feet or so, producing air above as we consume below. Its disadvantage for diving is that one must trail an air hose — here, around great cliffs of coral.

Underwater we find long rectangular blocks of rock lying parallel to each other with deep troughs between them. The tops are only a few feet from the surface; the bottoms lie between 20 and 30 feet down, and in some places even deeper. After a while we switch to snorkeling. In one place rock connects parallel blocks creating an arch about 20 tall. Beautiful corals are everywhere, and many reef fish.

Beautiful corals are everywhere, and many reef fish.

We circle Cockroach, another great dive spot about 200 feet west of George Dog, then we head for Great Dog. All the moorings on the west end of Great Dog are occupied, so we head for the south side and tie up to one of five very closely spaced moorings. We arrive as another boat pulls into the last mooring directly in front of us.

We snorkel here and find it very different from George Dog. There are no great cliffs. In fact, there are no rocks at all, but coral is everywhere in about 20 feet of water. The coral heads are large and colorful. They lie with one to three feet of the bottom, and seem to go on forever all along the south side. We see no sandy places where a boat could anchor here.

Later we dinghy around Great Dog and land on the beach on the north side. This is not an easy landing since coral is everywhere off the beach. We carefully maneuver our dinghy between heads and land without hitting anything. It is a nice short beach with piles of soft sand just off the shore.

...a nice short beach with piles of soft sand...

We climb over the rocks at each end. Turban shells are clustered in the tidal pools. We find this kind of shell in abundance on almost every beach in the Virgins; here we see them alive, in their natural habitat. Close to the beach we find an odd sort of cactus plant, one adorned on its top with a tuft of fuzz. We wonder what purpose such fuzz could serve. A cactus should be prickly!

A cactus should be prickly!

We continue around Great Dog in our dinghy, impressed by the sheer rock walls along several parts of its coastline. In one place, a 40-foot boulder has broken in two, providing through the resulting crack a view of a tiny cove on the other side.

...a 40-foot boulder has broken in two...

We continue on to the west end of the island. This time we find several moorings unoccupied. We note that boats tend to spend just an hour or so at a mooring, then move on. This is good, since there really is no place we have seen to anchor in the Dog Islands without killing coral. There is shallow and still water off the west end, with rocks popping up above the surface here and there.

...there is no good place...to anchor in the Dogs without killing coral.

We stop in our dinghy off the beach to the west of our mooring. This area is crowded with coral heads. We carefully navigate through the corals, standing in the dinghy and peering into the water, the sun behind us, but we cannot see a clear route to the beach, so we anchor in 5 feet of water in a sandy patch, carefully confirming that our anchor rode will not brush coral. We snorkel around in the shallow water. While there is no current, it is easy to become trapped with coral on three sides within inches of the surface and barely enough room to turn around. We feel a bit claustrophobic here.

Later in the afternoon we sail the seven miles to Maya Cove on the east side of Tortola. It is a delightful sail in a ten-knot wind with small seas. The views of the islands on all sides are spectacular as we sail southwest down Sir Francis Drake Channel. Ferries whiz by. We are surrounded by many sailboats, some sailing, some motoring in these light airs and gentle seas.

Ferries whiz by.

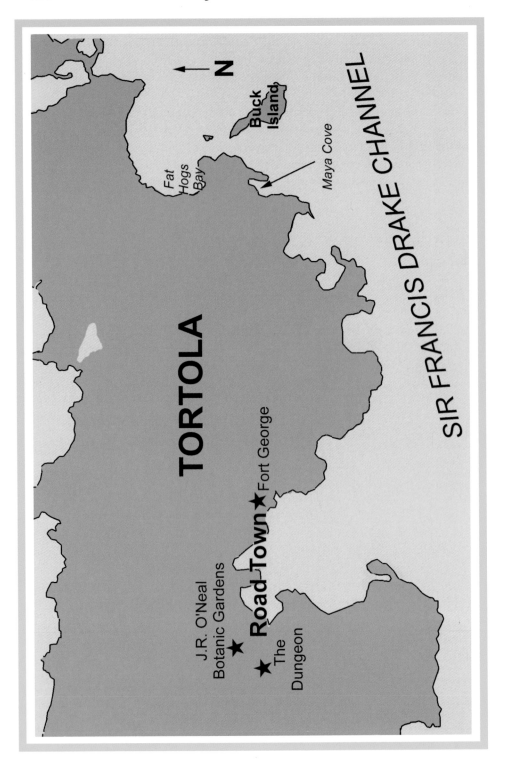

8: Road Town

We want to anchor off Buck Island, just to the north of Maya Cove on the east side of Tortola. We arrive around 6 o'clock, with nobody in the place we have chosen for the night's anchorage. We do not see the mooring buoys described in our guidebook. We drop our sails and motor around the south side of the island. The water is shallow, between 5 and 10 feet. We like the shallow water, but there are islets of coral everywhere. We need a 40-foot stretch of sand — no coral heads, please — to accommodate our 40 feet of chain rode that will lie on the bottom. Finding no such place, we move to Maya Cove and anchor between two empty mooring buoys. When we dive to check our anchor, we find we have put the anchor down well, about 20 feet upwind from a cable on the bottom connecting two buoys. When anchoring between mooring buoys we are always concerned about fouling submerged lines.

...we move to Maya Cove, and settle between two mooring buoys.

Shortly after we arrive, a large monohull shows up, piloted by a lone white-haired man wearing khaki trousers and a long-sleeved shirt. He grabs a mooring line that has a dinghy tied to it as well as a tangle of lines and buoys. Carefully he walks the dinghy back to the stern of his boat and ties it beside his dinghy. Then he begins to untangle the lines and buoys, tying each line off to his lifeline. It takes him a good half-hour and he does a tidy job of it. When he is finished, he goes below, probably, we think, to prepare his supper. We imagine that it will be a gourmet meal, with pinches of exotic spice, for here is a man who does things properly.

Maya Cove is home to two charter fleets, Sun Yacht Charters and Tropic Island Yacht Management. The harbor is full of large sailboats. We dinghy around admiring the boats, then later dinghy over to Buck Island. We attempt to go between Buck Island and Tortola to see Fat Hogs Bay and the settlement at East End up close, but it is too shoal even for our dinghy, even for drifting with our outboard motor tilted up out of the water.

In the morning, we motor *Top Cat* the few miles to Road Town in a dead calm. A high has settled in to the north of us and stopped the tradewinds. No sailing today. We feel much warmer without the steady wind. We anchor 10 feet of water off The Pub, a restaurant just north of the Fort Burt Marina.

Road Town is a busy small town. Traffic buzzes along its roads with little room on the shoulders for pedestrians. Buildings, highways, and homes are under construction. We walk cautiously as we sightsee. The city is the capital of BVI, and appears to be much more of a working town than Charlotte Amalie, which is focused on tourists. There is no old section of Road Town, as in Charlotte Amalie. But there are supermarkets and department stores, and a full range of marine supplies.

We visit the J.R. O'Neal Botanic Gardens. The gardens are maintained by the park service. They cover four lush acres. They feature a splendid grouping of ixoras of all colors and sizes, from tall to tiny, from white through pink, red, yellow, and orange. The cactus and succulent garden offers specimens we have seen on the slopes of the islands — the round cactus with a red knob on the top is turk's cap; the organ-pipe-type cactus we have seen so much of has the unfortunate name dildo. There is a native bush (medicinal herb) garden, a fernery, and an orchid-filled lattice-house. Here we also find a specimen of the Anegada acacia, a plant that is native to only one place in the world, Anegada, and we have been there!

...the J.R. O'Neal Botanic Gardens...

We take a dinghy ride around the harbor, starting at the Fort Burt Marina, looking for a good place to buy lunch. Fort Burt Marina has no restaurant, and appears to have no dinghy dock. We continue on, exploring the harbor. We pass a big government building and we pass many sailboats. We stop at the Village Cay Marina and Hotel restaurant near the center of town for lunch. The restaurant overlooks the marina, which like all other marinas here is filled with sailboats. The server is pleasant and helps us move the table and chairs to shelter when a sudden shower becomes a downpour.

This city is obviously too busy with the here-and-now to treasure its history. We stop at The Dungeon and at Fort George, both listed on the BVI Road Town road map as local sights, and discover that they are not maintained. Indeed, they are in danger of disappearing right off the island. The Dungeon, a notorious prison for slaves, is full of trash and covered by weeds, unmarked in any way. We talk to the man whose father owned the property around the dungeon. He recalls playing in it as a child and describes its arched ceiling. He says it goes back a hundred feet or more. He wants to clean it up and provide a historical marker — that sounds good to us. We walk miles to find the ruins of Fort George? (we can't be sure it's Fort George, but it's in the right place). It lies just uphill of a private house. A dog is chained to the front of the fort and an old car is parked behind it.

...The Dungeon...

...the ruins of Fort George?...

Our trip up the hill to find the fort gives us a good workout, but from the hillside we get splendid views of Road Town and its large and busy harbor.

...splendid views of Road Town...

We also stop at Her Majesty's Prison. According to the man at The Dungeon, there's a move afoot to use the old prison as an island museum now that Tortola is building a new jail. The prison is surrounded by white walls topped by barbed wire. We can see the peach-colored prison buildings beyond the encircling wall. Incongruously, a door knocker like the kind you'd find on the door of a family house has been installed on the red prison door. In addition, the tiny door-in-a-door that is meant to give access to the prison is padlocked. Apparently, you can't get out, but then you can't go in, either!

...Her Majesty's Prison.

The city is the headquarters for the Moorings charter fleet. We visit the moorings facility where we find charter sailboats of all sizes (except small). We stop for drinks at their restaurant/bar. Once again, we are pleasantly surprised by the kindness and thoughtfulness of the staff. We are hot and tired after our sightseeing trek: they show us to a quiet, cool spot near the swimming pool where the breeze blows through.

With the wind dead in the afternoon we decide we do not need to return to a hot boat. We will take a dinghy trip to cool off. We tour the waterfront and admire the large houses on the hillside. There are so many, and it seems to us, as native flatlanders, that they have taken such grave chances with the slope! Some are cantilevered at precarious angles. Others seem carved out of the rock, and appear to lack parking spaces. Still others have driveways so steep it seems likely that a car would tumble down them.

...they have taken such chances with the slope!

...about a dozen goats walking along the road...

As we turn around to come back to our anchorage, we spot a group of about a dozen goats walking along the road that parallels the coastline. They pick their way nimbly along the rocks, apparently migrating to better grazing grounds. Some of the cars slow, many do not. The goats appear to be on their way to downtown Road Town. What will they do when they get there? we wonder. Perhaps they will head uphill, among the trees and brush of the mountainside, before they are forced onto the busy streets.

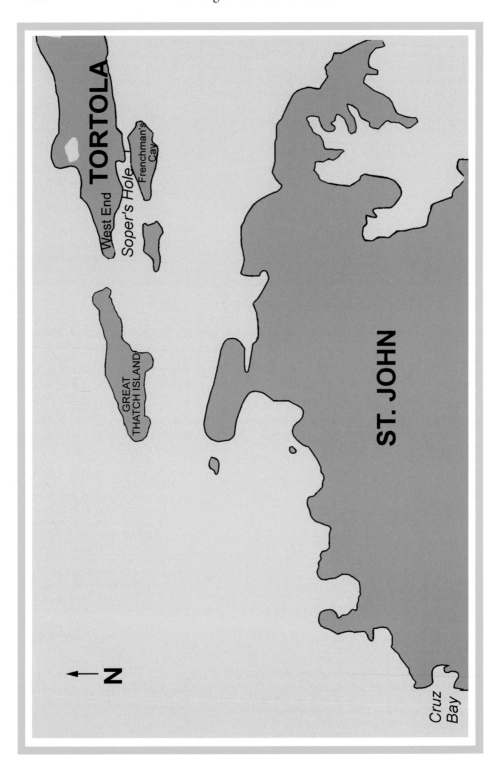

9: Back in the USVI

We leave Road Town early in a dead calm, headed for Great Thatch Island. It is a clear, calm, beautiful morning. We admire the houses on Tortola as we motor along the shoreline, heading south and west. Ferries pass enroute to U.S. waters. It is a delightful ride even with the engine on.

Ferries pass en route to U.S. waters.

Great Thatch is uninhabited. We see no other boats anchored along its shore when we arrive. A small white sand beach, protected by patch coral, adorns the south side of the island. We look for a sandy patch of bottom where we can throw down our hook. We require a circle of at least 60 feet in diameter in these shallows. We find no such patch here. We motor out to water 40 feet deep and drop our anchor there.

...no easy path to the beach.

We dinghy to shore, but find no easy path to the beach. Once again the coral has stymied our plans. The reef is dense, and close to the surface in several places, especially near shore. We decide to anchor the dinghy in a sandy patch at the eastern end of the beach next to a sheer rock cliff. From there we snorkel back to explore the reef. We tumble off the dinghy and gaze down on a terrain of rippled sand as white as sugar, which soon gives way to the dusty lace of old, broken coral. Bright-hued reef fish stand out against this beige background like jewels on velvet. Now we begin to see the first coral formations — tan brain corals, their spherical surfaces patterned with convoluted ridges. This place has many huge schools of inch-long silver fish. Repeatedly they form a clouds of glitter around us as we move along. At one point we swim steadily through such a school for several minutes.

We see stoplight parrot fish, gorgeous in green, blue, purple, and yellow. We see salmon-colored squirrelfish, with sawtooth fins. Several French angelfish, round and elegant in charcoal-gray with white trim, drift by. We pass large stands of elkhorn coral, with thick flat branches of yellowish-tan, and float over seafans of vivid purple.

We slide into the shallows, suddenly in inches of water, and sit up. We have reached the beach. We get to our feet to explore. The island is full of vegetation, with no evidence of man or goat.

Late in the morning we circle Great Thatch, heading for Soper's Hole to have lunch and to check out at BVI immigration. The anchorage deep inside Soper's Hole is crowded, but we find a good spot in 30 feet of water in the northeast corner. In front of us are a couple of very large sunken boats, and all around us are boats on moorings.

...Soper's Hole...

Soper's Hole is protected by Tortola to the north and Frenchman's Cay to the south. It ends in a narrow channel that passes to a harbor to the east. We explore, dinghying through the channel, which we discover is only slightly wider than a creek. It passes under a low bridge. A few knots of current make the trip somewhat tricky.

...a narrow channel that passes to a harbor to the east.

After our dinghy tour we stop at Soper's Hole Wharf & Marina for lunch at Pusser's Landing. We are beginning to realize that there are Pusser's installations everywhere in these islands. We have begun debating how to pronounce the word, as we have not yet heard it said. Is it Puss-(as in cat) urs? Or is it Pus (as nasty bodily fluid) urs? Or maybe even Poose-urs or Pooz-urs? We inquire at one of the stores in the Pusser's complex and learn that it is Pus-urs. No, the clerk says, Pusser is not somebody's name. It is a corruption of the word "person." This explanation makes a lot of sense. We have noticed that the people here in the island seem to speak two different languages. One is English, and we have no trouble understanding it, even in their lilting island accents. The second is a version of English so different from the original that only by carefully listening can we catch any of the words, let alone the meaning.

We have a flying fish sandwich with a very hot West Indian sauce, and a dolphin sandwich. We really like the Light Amstel beer so many of the island restaurants serve, so we each have one and then share a third. We explore the stores and do a little shopping, then pause to take pictures of the handsome dock area, with the backdrop of lush tropical isalnds.

...the handsome dock area, with the backdrop of lush tropical isalnds.

West End on Soper's Hole is one of the four official points of entry and departure for the BVI. We dinghy to the ferry dock during a lull in the ferry service to check out. The process is very simple, and we are done and leaving in minutes.

Without status, temporarily people without a country, we head for U.S. waters. Soon we are at Cruz Bay on St. John. We pick up a mooring, free here in the USVI. This is a crowded harbor, chock full of small local boats on both public and private moorings. We do not feel secure anchored here with other boats so close, so we need a mooring to stay the night. We feel very fortunate when we find an unused public mooring, though the mooring buoy is dingy and we are at first unsure whether this a private mooring with its marking obscured. We ask a local live-aboard yachtie if the mooring is public. He confirms that it is.

We dinghy to the dinghy dock at the U.S. National Park Service Visitor Center. From there we walk the short distance to the Customs and Immigration center, and check officially back into the United States. Home at last. Cruz Bay is busy, crowded, noisy, dusty, and the air is thick with exhaust fumes from the morass of cars, boats, and ferries, all in a hurry. The ferries are the worst offenders — some depositing passengers, others disgorging vehicles and cargo, distributing clouds of hydrocarbons. Tourists crowd the narrow sidewalks on their way to duty-free upscale stores where they will buy jewelry, perfume, liquor, and fashions. The residents mill among many small stall-type stores that sell food, fruit, drinks on the bayfront.

We tour the park visitor center, where we watch an 18-minute film that includes much of the islands' history, from the sad chronicle of the first inhabitants, passive Arowak and man-eating Caribe Indians; to Columbus's discovery of the islands; to Danish sugarcane plantations and slavery; to current problems with reef damage. If it isn't ferocious people-eating Indians or money-grubbing slave-owning Danes, it's careless snorkelers and boaters. Even paradise has problems.

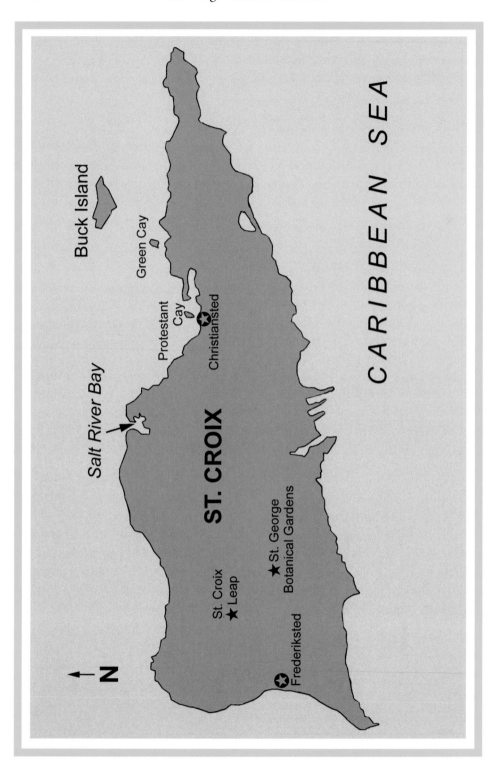

10: St. Croix

We are glad to leave the bustle of Cruz Bay the next morning for the long trip across the water to the island of St. Croix, 35 miles south. The winds are light with little sea as we depart at 6:30. As we pass Dog Island southwest of Little St. James Island we see a ribbon of rainbow trailing from a storm cloud. We put up our sails, expecting the winds to increase steadily through the morning. By 9 o'clock we have 10 knots of wind and we are sailing at a speed of over 5 knots. By lunch we have all the wind we need, and are hoping no more will be forthcoming. The winds continue to rise, however, and the ocean grows bumpy. The lunch-maker complains bitterly from the galley and threatens mayhem unless the captain gets the seas under control.

...we see a ribbon of rainbow...

We reach Christiansted Harbor at 1 o'clock. The wind disappears as we motor into the lee of the island. We note that the 180 foot radio tower at Ft. Louise Augusta is gone. The radio tower is on our chart and in our guidebook, but we don't need it for navigation, because this harbor is well marked with buoys. We motor in, following the path laid out by the lines of green and red marker buoys – they are a newfangled kind, composed of plastic, with solar panels to power their lights at night. The harbor is protected by reefs; in the afternoon sun we easily spot them as lighter areas, with some breaking waves. We pass Fort Christiansvern, a handsome yellow building that overhangs the rocky shoreline, and we pass Protestant Cay to starboard. We see a few dozen sailboats all anchored west of the cay, and decide to anchor at the far end of the pack, well away from the local boats that dominate the anchorage.

...Fort Christiansvaern, a handsome yellow building...

We anchor in the shallow part of the harbor, in 7 feet of water over a sandy bottom. As we move back on our rode, we discover that our boat passes near the wreckage of a sunken boat. The wreck looks as if it could lie within a few feet of the surface. Concerned about the possibility of hitting the wreck as we swing at anchor, we decide to move. Our new anchorage is also well separated from our neighbors. We are behind them and still far enough from shore for quiet and privacy. We are near the channel, however, and this gives us a front-row seat for the takeoffs and landings of the Christiansted seaplane that flies between here and St. Thomas and the slow progress of a barge being moved into the harbor near the big generating plant by a tugboat.

There are no charter boats here! We see local boats, and some day-charter boats, but no boats from the charter fleets in the islands to our north. The 35

...the Christiansted seaplane...

...a tugboat guiding a barge into the harbor...

miles of sea that separate this island from the rest must be a major factor in their absence. A little rough weather and it's an unpleasantly bouncy trip for people who have come here for sailing fun. Also, it takes most of a day for a sailboat to make the round trip and charter boaters are probably reluctant to spend precious charter time in long passages.

We dinghy over to see Fort Christiansvaern and the town of Christiansted. We tie up at the public dock near the fort, next to two decrepit dinghies. Both are thoroughly secured with cables, chains, and locks. We worry about our dinghy, which is only tied to a cleat, but we leave it anyway to tour the fort.

...cannons pointing out to sea.

The fort is relatively small, but in remarkably good condition. It has three separate dungeon areas — discipline was apparently a serious problem for the early Danish military. According to a sign, the dungeons were also used to hold escaped slaves until they could be claimed by their owners. In one, some poor prisoner carved what appears to be the sketch of buildings into the plank floor. The dungeons have ceilings that are so low only the tiniest man could stand upright in them, a design that served to both punish and control the prisoner. On the rooftop stands a row of cannons pointing out to sea. They look jaunty and decorative, thought they are clearly aimed at pleasure boaters out in the harbor.

We go outside again and read a historical marker explaining that Alexander Hamilton lived near the fort as a boy. We meet the local park ranger, who encourages us to visit the island's famous rainforest, even though the weather has been dry and it isn't as lush as usual. We ask about Buck Island at the eastern tip of the island; great snorkeling, he says, with good anchorages near the beach.

We walk around the town. We visit many shops, all in narrow alleyways. It is a picturesque town with narrow one-way streets and many restaurant/bars

It is a picturesque town...

and shops. Most of the streets are one-way, but the buildings do not appear as old as in St. Thomas. We reserve a rental car for the next morning.

In the morning we dinghy to the St. Croix Marina, where we are met by a rental car employee and driven to the rental-car agency. We are issued a car and set off for our tour, heading to the southwest part of the island. On the way we pass by an enormous oil refinery. We now understand the purpose of the large industrial port at Limetree Bay on the south side of the island, which is shown on our navigational chart.

We arrive at the St. George Botanical Garden in mid-morning, and are very impressed with its size and beauty. Many of the plant collections use the ruins of the old sugarcane plantation buildings as a backdrop. We admire the orchids spotted here and there around the gardens, the pretty flower garden surrounding an old masonry house, bromeliads with their exotic spikes of flowers, the many tropical trees and bushes in bloom.

Our next stop is the island K-Mart, a very popular local store. Ah, brightly lit, wide-aisled, air-conditioned K-Mart! We really feel at home. The store has brand names we know, and a familiar layout. At this K-Mart's Islander Café, however, we see some differences. Besides the usual burger and fries, the menu offers stewed goat, curried chicken, and something called saltfish. We order seasoned chicken and rice and a kingfish platter. The plates are piled high. The food is surprisingly low-cost and very flavorful.

As we shop, we are wowed by the fashion sense of the island ladies around us in the store. Wherever we have gone in the Virgin Islands, women are finely attired. Fat or thin, tall or short, old or young, conservative or trendy, they dress with a real feeling for color, style, and fit. Many wear coordinating skirt-and-blouse combinations. Hats are surprisingly popular.

We make our way around to Fredriksted on the west coast. It has a very large cruise ship pier, but we see no cruise ships today. The town seems smaller than Christiansted, and is in a state of intense renovation, with piles of construction materials and rubble everywhere. Fort Frederik, a large red building with white shutters, is being repainted. Workers swarm between, around, over, and on top of the buildings in the area. Heavy equipment moves back and forth, pushing dirt and rock hither and yon. We can see that the area will be quite grand when ass the work is done. We promise ourselves to return someday and see how it turns out.

...Fort Frederik...

...piles of construction materials and rubble everywhere...

Later in the afternoon we drive through the dry rainforest. As described by the park ranger earlier, we find it dry, but also full of tropical bird songs and large trees and tropical plants. We stop at a 150-foot dam that holds back no water but enables us to see for ourselves how tall these trees really are.

...a 150-foot dam...

We stop at St. Croix Leap where a group of woodworkers carve mahogany and other exotic hardwoods into sculptures, plaques, clocks, hand mirrors, end tables, and other items to sell to tourists. The road to the workshop is lined on both sides with wood, big lengths of tree trunk still covered with bark, thick branches, and even, we are pleased to see, a big pile of old utility poles. The workshop is a barnlike building crammed with woodworking tools and machinery, pieces of wood, and projects in progress. Several large dogs snooze on the floor of this big, airy space. A back corner of the workshop has been reserved for displaying merchandise. We purchase a tiny wooden refrigerator magnet in the shape of a turtle and a very expensive set of kitchen utensils (salad fork and spoon, and two other items whose use escapes us) in a beautifully turned wooden holder.

...at St. Croix Leap ...the road...is lined on both sides with wood...

The workshop is ...crammed with woodworking tools and machinery...

The only worker here is listening to the radio as he carves. The radio voice is familiar. We have heard this voice before, a man with an island accent who is the Virgin Islands' answer to Rush Limbaugh, except that his theme is self-improvement. He exhorts his listeners to stay in school, to have the courage of their convictions, to read and heed Bible teachings, to obey the law, to be clean, courteous, and righteous. He applauds good citizenship, going on to describe local examples in detail. Many times we go into stores or pass by cars with radios on, and The Exhorter is talking. He never breaks for a commercial, or even, for that matter, a breath. His listeners seem entranced by his message. It is a captivating one.

We make our way back home along the coast, where the beach is continuous. The scene is vaguely reminiscent of the Big Sur drive along the California coast, except that the water breaks on white sand beaches instead over rocks. We like St. Croix — it is hilly enough to be scenic but not so mountainous that the heart is constantly in the mouth while traveling the roads. It is large enough to have an economy separate from tourism. It has beautiful beaches and splendid protected anchorages. It seems to have solved the feral livestock problem that plagues the other islands. We have seen no free-ranging goats, cattle, or donkeys on St.Croix. We have seen a small flock of cattle, fenced in with

...it is hilly enough to be scenic...

barbed wire, and a huge flock of sheep in a faraway pasture. But no endlessly *ma-a-a-ahing* goats in the hills, no donkeys glaring at us from well-worn trails, no clattering herds of scrawny cattle.

Only Christiansted and Fredericksted have any size. However, many small settlements are scattered through the hills. We pass through areas marked on the map with intriguing names — Wheel of Fortune, Punch, Upper Love, Jealousy, Humbug, Body Slob, Hope, Blessing, Barren Spot, Rust Up Twist, Diamond, Pearl, and Stony Ground. We can't help speculating about what inspired these interesting place names.

We return our rental car by closing time so we can depart for our next destination at first light in the morning instead of leaving after we have turned it in. The night is cool and despite a bright moon, we have a two-minute rain that forces us to close every hatch in the boat.

In the morning we vacate our pleasant Christiansted anchorage and head east for Buck Island Reef National Monument, an island and its surrounding reef at the eastern tip of the island. We leave early so we can travel at the time of lightest wind, since we will be traveling directly to windward. For about an hour we motor into the wind, waves, and sun. At last we reach our destination and anchor off a sandy beach in about 10 feet of water at the west end of the island. Two sailboats, neither a charterboat, are already here.

...we ...anchor off a sandy beach in about 10 feet of water...

We have an early lunch and watch the parade of boats arriving as we eat. This is Sunday, a day for fun for both locals and tourists, and we see both in abundance. Agile little sailboats zip in and around us; a giant catamaran loaded with sightseers anchors just off the beach; a motorboat anchors behind us. A boat captain, so black he seems like a shadow on the deck of his very white sailboat, scurries about anchoring, putting up a sunshade, breaking out snorkeling gear. His pale-skinned passengers sit like stones, watching as he rushes from task to task. At last, all is in readiness. The passengers drop one by one into the water to go ashore or to snorkel, and he finally gets to sit down on deck, dangling his feet in the turquoise sea. Soon enough they will all be returning for the trip back to St. Croix.

We take a dinghy-and-snorkel trip around the island, traveling counterclockwise. The west and south sides of the island are all smooth, sandy beach. But as we travel around to the east we see a long line of reef, its topmost part above water, several hundred feet off shore. At the southeast end a break in the reef is marked with a green buoy to guide boats in. Inside the enclosing reef the water is less than 10 feet deep, and very calm. The island's shore is mostly rock here. Its cactus-covered slopes rise several hundred feet.

The lagoon at the southeast end of the reef has a single occupant, a motorboat. We continue on to the northeast end. There we find a collection of moorings maintained by the National Park Service. This area is for snorkeling only. Diving is not permitted here, nor is it worthwhile in these shallow waters. The moorings are for small boats, although we see big tourist-carrying catamarans and private sailboats as large as 30 feet tied to moorings.

We tie up to one of the moorings and snorkel. Underwater signs have been installed that are meant to help the snorkeler identify the various kinds of tropical fish, coral, and other undersea creatures. However, the signs seem randomly placed, like some great force lifted them from their original location and dumped them back, to rest in disarray wherever they have fallen. On the other hand, since most of the markers identify fish there really is no appropriate scheme for placement.

The water is the perfect depth for a snorkeler, never more than about seven feet, near enough the attractions to see them but far enough away not to become ensnared in them. But away from the mooring area there are reefs within inches off the surface of the water, and breaking surf. Tall, branching elkhorn corals reach toward the water's surface like opening hands.

The corals stand out well against patches of very white sand. With the crystal-clear water and a wide variety of reef fish, we really enjoy our snorkeling time. This area, amongst the moorings, seems to be very safe, with no corals within easy reach, and no significant currents. It seems a very good place for an underwater trail.

Back in the dinghy we continue with the intent of completely circling the island. The protective fringing reef continues on the north side a few hundred feet offshore. But the farther we travel west, the more the waters between it and the shore are crowded with patch reefs. We pilot the dinghy standing up,

...elkhorn corals reach for the surface...

an extension on the tiller, watching carefully for shallow areas, and motor at idle. We spot a small sand beach on the north shore, with rocky beaches and rock cliffs everywhere else. The northwest end of the passage proves most difficult, but not as difficult as the north side of Anegada. We emerge through the fringing reef at the west; here the shore is sand.

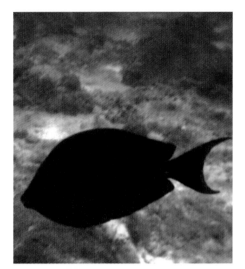 

...a wide variety of reef fish...

The fringing reef with shallow water near the shore and the extensive beach on the west and south shore are reminiscent of Anegada. Yet here there are steep slopes, and many different kinds of rocks.

Later we take a second snorkeling trip and meet up with a large barracuda. It comes unusually close and it seems unafraid. The light conditions are perfect, so we take some underwater pictures of our companion. It stays close, posing politely, clearly interested in us. Despite an ominous appearance (that menacing stare, that thrust-out jaw!), the barracudas we have met in Florida waters have invariably been friendly and curious. The same is true, it seems, of Virgin Island barracudas.

...we...meet up with a large barracuda.

Renegade, a large catamaran loaded with tourists, pulls up to a mooring. We observe that among these tourists, many are beginning snorkelers. We snorkel for a bit with the tourists, and take a picture of the boat from the water's surface. Soon everyone is back aboard and *Renegade* leaves.

We busy ourselves with boat chores and about 3 in the afternoon we head for shore again, intending to explore the island's interior. We follow a trail that winds up from the south side of the island to the summit, 330 feet above the sea, and then back down to the northwest. At the start of the trail near the

...a large catamaran loaded with tourists...

picnic benches is a warning sign that identifies the poisonous manchioneel tree (don't eat its fruit, don't even stand under its dripping branches for shelter from the rain!).

The identifying tree itself is gone. Only a stump remains. We decide to avoid all trees we can't identify, and in fact this is fairly easy since there are very few trees on the trail. It is a hot climb through arid terrain, but the trail, though steep, is cleared and we have only to sidestep branches here and there. We see many varieties of cacti. The larger and taller ones are festooned with bromeliads and orchid plants. The few orchid blooms we see look like those growing on the limbs of the brushy trees on Anegada. Here also are white and pink lantana bushes, frangipani trees with their swirled white blooms, thorny acacias with tiny yellow powderpuffs for flowers.

On our way up, we have a splendid view of Buck Island's southern reef and St. Croix on the other side of the channel. From this vantage point we can see the motorboat we saw earlier on our dinghy trip, anchored inside the reef . It is a

...the motorboat...anchored inside the reef.

protected spot with plenty of depth, but it must take some courage, we think, to trust the markers that show the narrow passage through the reef.

When we reach the island's summit we look out on a good view of the north shore. A heap of lumber, apparently the remains of a wooden observation platform, rests to one side. A fallen sign half covered by brush reads "Limit: 15 Persons." We speculate that the limit must have been exceeded — hence, the heap. From our lookout we can watch frigatebirds gliding upward on thermals. The big birds are wafted ever higher, spiraling to a point level with us, then higher and higher over our heads until they are specks above us at which point they suddenly decide to start over and dive down to sea level to begin anew their upward glide.

We head down the trail to the other side of the island. This section of the trail does not see much use, we soon discover. It is seriously overgrown. Repeatedly, thorny acacia branches reach out to catch our clothes, our arms, our legs, and we lose track of the trail route when the going gets especially tough. We continue doggedly downhill and emerge at last at a sandy beach that is marked by tiny flags every foot or so. It appears to us that the rangers are keeping track of shoreline erosion with this palisade of markers.

...frigatebirds gliding upward on the thermals...

There are many pelicans on this beach, lounging around on the sand, perched on dead trees and in the rocks. We try not to disturb them as we follow a shoreline route back to our dinghy.

...many pelicans...

We follow the beach around the point and discover people everywhere — on the beach, in the water, on boats, under the water. Buck Island, it seems, is the place to be on a sunny Sunday.

We pass turtle tracks in the sand. We know that sometimes Florida sea turtles come ashore to lay their eggs but go back again without doing so and wonder what happened here. This seems like a poor beach for turtle nests to us. Once you get far enough up the beach to be well above the high-tide mark, the sand gets thin over the rocky core of the island. Hard to dig a hole in rock.

...turtle tracks...

Later, back at the boat, we drink gin-and-tonics and watch the local boats depart for St. Croix. They leave one by one until our only company is a small local trawler, tied up at the park dock. It looks like it will be a breezy night with a bright moon, fine for sleeping. Once again we are grateful for the absence of bugs in these islands. Only twice have we had to close up the boat at night.

Morning brings heavier seas and stronger winds. *Top Cat* is rocking. We pull up our anchor and move the boat slightly inshore. It is tricky choosing the right place. Too far off, and we have waves, boat motion, and a rocky bottom. Too far in, and we have no cooling breezes.

We dinghy ashore for a walk on the beach. It is Monday, and the island is deserted. The picnic grounds on the point, crammed with people yesterday, are empty. The picnickers have cleaned up well after themselves. The garbage cans provided for trash are filled, but not so much as a scrap of paper or empty soda can litters the grounds.

Later, we dinghy around to the moorings again, this time through heavy seas, to go snorkeling on the main reef. But the water is rough and we decide to return to the quieter side of the island and snorkel there. Remnants of an old reef, pockmarked reddish limestone, lie broken in pillow-shaped pieces just under the water. The water is only a couple of feet deep, and not as clear as the area around the moorings. There are also many patches of sea grass. Reef fish are everywhere. We see fairy basselets, front half purple, back half yellow. Rock beauties, sergeant majors, and four-eye butterflyfish dart in and out of small caves in the rock. Close to shore we pass a West Indian sea egg, a large purplish-skinned sea urchin covered with short white spines. It seems tightly molded, almost warped, into the top of a rounded rock. A school of several hundred foot-long fish swirls around us. Jacks, we think.

We climb out of the sea and sit for a time on the deserted beach, watching a fisherman whose craft is rigged for sailing.

...a fisherman whose craft is rigged for sailing.

...a catboat...

We have circled Buck Island by dinghy and we have climbed to its top. At about four in the afternoon we decide that the time has come to attempt a walk-around along its sometimes rocky, sometimes sandy shoreline. We are not sure if a complete circuit of the island is possible, but we intend to try. We follow the sandy beach of the picnic area around to the east until it becomes rock, and set out to circle the island counterclockwise.

The sheer cliffs of Buck Island appear to be made of shale. Layered like fine pastry, tilted up on end, the cliffsides are coming apart all around the island. The fallen pieces have been washed smooth by the sea, creating a beach of pebbles. This rocky beach averages only about a yard in width, in some places more, in a few places a lot less. Features we saw from our dinghy prove to be rather commonplace when seen close up. A flag we saw waving in the breeze turns out to be a plastic bag that has caught on the thorns of an acacia bush. A large sign resolves itself into the top of a white plastic cooler, washed high up into the rocks and wedged in well. We find a shoe stuck over a rusted steel reinforcing rod, many large pieces of timber, a hatch cover, lots of little floats and lengths of frayed plastic line in hues of red, blue, and green. We make it more than halfway around Buck Island before we run into a section of collapsed cliff that stops any further progress. More ambitious hikers (or those willing to get their shoes wet) would doubtless have completed the circuit.

A kite... flying ahead of it.

We watch a sailboat pass, a catboat, with the mast far forward. It really is a pretty craft. A kite connected to its mast is flying ahead of it. What purpose this can serve we discuss for some time. Does the kite help pull the boat? We doubt it. Perhaps the kite is carrying a camera aloft, and these people are recording their trip from above. If so, they have chosen a bad time for it. The sun has gone away. It looks as if we are in for some rain.

We return to *Top Cat* in a slight drizzle. The trawler that shared our anchorage has gone by the time we get back A sunset sail-by of *Renegade* gives us some company for a while. And then we are alone, anchored in isolation for the first time on our Virgin Island vacation.

In the morning we put up our mainsail, pull up our anchor, and roll open the jib. We drift off on the wind, then as we round the southwest corner of the island, we pick up the full force of the wind. *Top Cat* almost jumps out of the water, thrusting forward under the full force of 20-knot tradewinds. We head south for a close look at St. Croix shoreline, then west to Green Cay, then out north past the Scotch Bank. It is a breezy, sunny day, and we are sailing in paradise. We head west along the coast of St. Croix for Salt River Bay, the spot where Columbus landed on his second voyage to the New World in 1493.

After a hour or so we turn north of Whitehorse Rock, drop the sails, and head into Salt River Bay. There are reefs on both sides of the entrance, easily spotted because of the breaking waves. Outside of the shallow reefs are National Park Service moorings. We see a diveboat filled with divers pull up to one. The entrance to the bay is also marked, with a green can buoy as indicated on our chart. We enter and are immediately in shallow water. We head a little east to avoid rocks directly to our south, then turn back south toward the boats anchored ahead of us. At one point we pass over water that is only five feet deep. The water is murky. This bay is a saltwater estuary, and the bottom is mostly sand and grasses.

We anchor near the front of the pack...

We circle the boats in the harbor looking for the best place to anchor. Half the boats are on private moorings and most of the rest are anchored. We see only a handful of park moorings, or what we think are park moorings. Several are not being used, but they are far too close to other boats for our taste. We anchor in 10 feet of water, near the front of the pack where we will get a good breeze.

After we are settled in we begin our circumnavigation of the bay by dinghy. We first pass through the pack of boats. Clearly most are permanent residents, and quite a few of these are barely floating wrecks or fully sunken wrecks. One large old sailboat, sans mast and rigging, laid out on its side on the mangroves, has two audacious KEEP-OFF signs posted, as if it were the pride of the fleet!   A huge old mastless and stripped-down sailboat near where we are anchored is decorated with carved wooden dragons fore and aft, and along its topsides. We are soon past the intact vessels and continue to the south end of the harbor, where boats have become submarines. They wallow among the wreckage of dead mangroves, both boats and mangroves victims of hurricane Marilyn in 1995.

...dead mangroves...

We see several birds among the bleached mangrove roots and limbs. They are skittish about having their photographs taken. We cut the dinghy motor and try to float closer, but many attempts end in failure when a bird flies off just as we get close enough to snap a picture.

...birds among the ...mangroves...

We continue around to the mangroves near the marina and spot a colony of nesting cattle egrets. Cattle egrets are plentiful in Florida, but we have never seen a nesting colony. Some of the nestlings, nearly full grown, stand bravely erect or struggle for space in nests that have become far too small for them.

Others, still tiny balls of fluff, are hunkered down, busy sleeping and growing. They ignore us and we are pleased to be able to get close enough to take some good pictures, more than making up for the shy birds in the dead mangroves.

...nesting cattle egrets...

We stop at the marina for lunch. We ask where the Salt River Bay National Historic Site is located. It is right here, they say, but add that the historic marker that described Columbus's landing was destroyed by Marilyn. The U.S. Park Service has no presence here. Dive shop and marina employees answer questions and supply all necessary information. They appear to have no interest in a greater role for the Park Service, or in encouraging tourists to visit the place as a historic site. They feel that the bay is an important saltwater sanctuary, and it should remain in its natural and undisturbed state, not a bad approach to preservation. Back in Florida, the emphasis on accessibility and tourism has too often led to ruin.

After lunch we continue our circumnavigation of the bay. We start at the beach on the western side north of the marina, which is protected by very shallow water. The bottom is turtle grass, very important as a breeding ground for fish. We paddle ashore, then walk the beach. We continue north until we are at Columbus Beach on the north shore. Here the beach is torn by rough surf, and the water is opaque, yet people are happily swimming.

...people are happily swimming.

We return to our boat and cross the bay to the north side. There are two separate bays, one with several anchored boats, and another with many more dead mangroves, and some young and thriving trees. Blooming Spanish bayonets bring Columbus and his men to mind. What did they see when they came ashore here?

Blooming Spanish bayonets...

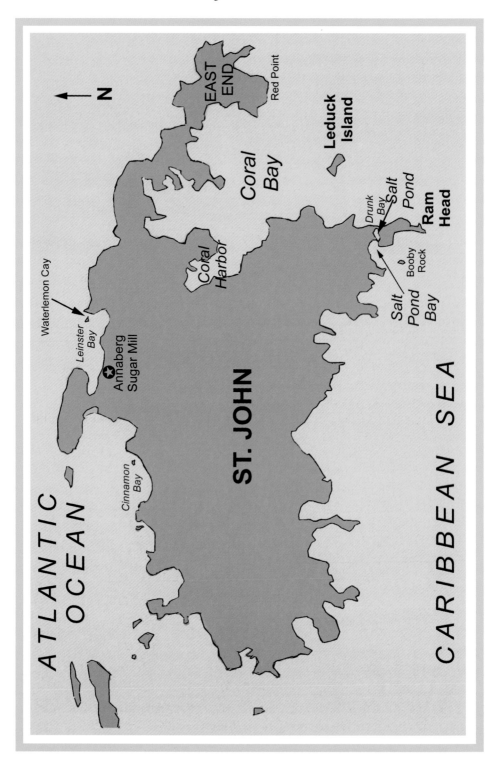

11: Back to St. John

We leave St. Croix early in the morning for St. John. Leaving, we pass a little farther off the rocks on the west side of the bay and see no less than 6 feet of water anywhere along our path. The wind is already at 17 knots a little after 6:30 and the seas are 5 to 7 feet. We are glad to be headed north and not directly into the waves and seas. Sailing with a single reef, at times we slow to a few knots. We are continually lofted high and then dropped low as big rollers move under us. Some of them break over our bow and splash us in the cockpit. Late in the morning the wind picks up to 20 knots or so. We remain relatively tight on the wind, so our progress is slow.

Around noon we arrive off Salt Pond Bay, *Top Cat*'s hull glittering with salt crystals. The rollers are huge. Even miles away we can see them crash against the rocky shore in blazes of white. There are no other boats here, but the bay is full of snorkeling tourists. Grabbing a mooring, we tie up, glad to stop for a while to have some lunch and a couple of beers.

...Salt Pond...

After lunch we dinghy to shore and see Salt Pond, then take the trail to the 200-foot summit of the rocky point of Ram Head. The trail winds through

...the trail to the 200-foot summit of the rocky point of Ram Head.

scrubby trees and brush, then over a beach formed of gray and white granite rocks and white corals, then up to clifftop over desert-like, rocky terrain. The section of trail over the beach is marked here and there with piles of rocks and large arrows formed by laying out hunks of coral in straight lines. Hundreds of turk's cap cacti cover the cliffs, along with acacias, scorpiontail, and a yellow-flowered plant that smells like eucalyptus. In many places the vegetation is only a foot high.

The...trail...is marked with piles of rocks...

...desert-like, rocky terrain...

Hundreds of turk's cap cacti cover the cliffs...

We reach the Ram Head summit and the view is spectacular! Surf thunders and boils on the rocky beach far below us and sailboats glide over shimmering waters in the far distance.

...the view is spectacular!

On the return trip back down the trail, we keep our camera at the ready and watch for birds. We spot perhaps a dozen hummingbirds, several yellow warblers, many bananaquits, and numerous thrashers. We try to photograph them, with mixed success. The bananaquits and hummingbirds are very fast and flitty. We watch transfixed as a small black bird with a thick beak eats seeds from a seedpod that it grasps elegantly in its claw.

...several yellow warblers...

...many bananaquits...

Back at the beach, we take a second trail to Drunk Bay past Salt Pond. The trail is short, and ends at a wide rock beach. The trail north along the shore from this beach is lined with turk's cap cacti and is covered with low brush. Oddly, the area reminds us of a Scottish moor.

Late in the afternoon we snorkel in Salt Pond Bay. This is a perfect place for children and beginning snorkelers, with clear water, sandy beaches, and rocky shores at both ends of the beach. Schools of very small fish are everywhere in these waters. One group of snorkelers near us calls out excitedly about a sea-turtle sighting. We do not see the turtle, but we pass two blue angelfish wildly chasing each other and two 4-inch grunts with mouths open rushing toward each other like dueling bighorn sheep. They don't bang heads but seem to be threatening to eat each other, although clearly their mouths are far too small for such an undertaking. We see many squirrelfish, parrotfish, and other reef fish, despite the fact that there are no large protective coral formations here, just rocks with some corals. Perhaps this little bay is a shelter from the wild waters beyond, and these fish are just visiting.

In the morning we motor around Ram Head, past Leduck Island, and into Coral Bay. Leduck Island is beautiful, but landing is prohibited to protect birds that nest there. Coral Harbor in the northwest corner of the bay is full of local boats and a few cruisers. We motor past Hurricane Hole in the north part of Coral Bay. We see no white sand beaches here, but the area is scenic with rocky cliffs and pebble beaches. There are also little bays here lined with mangroves, particularly in Hurricane Hole.

We continue motoring around Red Point and East End, finally out of Coral Bay, and on the east end of St. John. We pull out the jib, sailing slowly around the island until we reach Leinster Bay. We anchor in 20 feet of water and relax over a lunch of sandwiches and beer. We watch a three-masted Coast Guard sailboat drift by. What, we wonder, is the Coast Guard doing with a big old sailboat?

...a three-masted Coast Guard sailboat...

Leinster is a large, well-protected bay. There are a number of park service moorings, but more boats are anchored here than are moored.

Intent on touring the Annaberg Sugar Mill ruins, we dinghy to the beach. As our dinghy approaches the beach we see a sea turtle, a hawksbill, we think, and later we hear snorkelers in the area exclaiming loudly to each other as they, too, spot this graceful creature. We follow a gravel path along the Leinster Bay shoreline watching bananaquits and hummingbirds flit back and forth along the way. A donkey walks this path, too. We have seen him from the boat, and now we see his droppings. A constant stream of people travel the path. They park their cars at the lot near the sugar-mill ruins and walk to the beach to snorkel. The walk is about a half-mile long, breezy, and cool.

A donkey walks this path, too. We have seen him from the boat.

We pay $4 each to visit the plantation and spend about a half hour touring it. We spot a mongoose rushing along the roadside near the ticket booth, and take its picture. Though we have seen several of these animals in the islands, but this is the first one we have actually captured on film. They are not natives; the Danes brought them to kill rats on the sugar plantations.

The plantation ruins are of masonry construction. We recall what we learned about the local mortar — lime mixed with molasses — at the St. George Botanical Gardens. We wonder if a molasses-and-lime mortar was used here.

...a mongoose, rushing along the roadside..

Whatever the mortar, it holds together an eclectic mixture of materials: big angular green and gray stone, red and yellow bricks, and chunks of white coral. Corners and right angles around windows and doorways, and where two walls meet, are created by blocks of coral carved to fit, or by bricks. In some places the old construction has been repaired. A lighter mortar holds bits and pieces of rock that look pasted on.

Interpretive signs scattered through the site describe the functioning of a sugar mill fully, if briefly. In the 1700s, the wooded hills around this area were cleared and terraced; sugarcane formed a lush 6-foot-tall sea of grass over the slopes. The slaves who planted, tended, and harvested the cane, and worked in the sugar mill, lived in the simplest possible dwellings — lean-tos made of

They hauled the harvested cane to the windmill.

...the boiling room...

sticks and mud. After planting and harvesting, slaves hauled the cane to the windmill. Grinders inside, moved by gears attached to great sails at the windmill's top, crushed the cane to pulp. The sails could be turned in any direction to catch the wind when it changed. On calm days, a horse would turn a cane press in a yard nearby, doing the same job more expensively. (The windmill replaced the horse — except for calm days — in the early 1800s, a great technological advance.)

The juice of the cane, drained off, was taken to the boiling room, a large (now roofless) building at Annaberg. There it was boiled down over and over again, until it was a viscous liquid. Then it was set out to cool and crystallize into sugar. The boiling had to be stopped at exactly the right stage. If removed too soon, the liquid became and stayed molasses.

Around the corner from the boiling room is the spot where the plantation's still once stood. Here, fermented molasses was boiled in a big pot. The vapor from this cooking was run out through copper tubing, which was water-cooled. The vapor was thus distilled to liquid rum. The rum was aged for several years before it was sold. Sugar, molasses, rum — the sugarcane plantation had plenty of product, but its profitability depended on slave labor. The Virgin Island cane business did not survive the emancipation of the slaves in 1836. Annaberg and all the other plantations eventually closed down.

We trudge back to our boat, a little hot and a very tired of man's inhumanity to man. We decide to cool off with a snorkel around Waterlemon Cay. We leave our dinghy anchored in the channel defined by the green and red buoys leading to the Cay on its west side. As we head north around the tiny island, the water deepens. Here is a cascade of large, angular rocks, forming the basis for the reef. We see more and more corals, sponges, and sea fans. We see tropical fish — trunkfish, tiny striped sergeant majors, four-eyed butterflyfish, and parrotfish. Bar jacks, with intense blue lines outlining their backs, spin by us. Black, long-spined sea urchins bristle from crevices between the rocks.

At the north end of the cay we pick up a little swell from the sea, and the water within a few feet of the shore plunges swiftly to blue deeps of 15 feet and more. Much larger coral formations grow here, including pillar corals, star corals, and sea whips. On the east side the bottom gradually slopes up. There we are followed for some time by a two-foot long fish just a few inches below the surface. After it leaves, we enter a huge school of tiny fish. We pass through the school, seeing very little else, for several minutes, emerging over a coral pasture, where nibbling parrotfish are busy processing coral into beach sand. Our park informational brochure mentions a study that showed that the parrotfish grazing on an acre of coral reef produce a ton of sand every year.

We continue around the very shallow water at the south end of Waterlemon Cay and head back to our dinghy. Waterlemon is a very good snorkeling area, offering both calm shallow water and much deeper and rougher water with grander displays. We still prefer Cinnamon Bay where it's possible to enter the water from a white sandy beach and the sights are a short swim away.

We return to our boat to clean up and then sit outside and enjoy the scenery. A large sailboat anchored directly in front of us appears to be a crewed charter boat. It is laden with toys – kayaks, a sailboard — and an energetic woman and man appear to be handling most of the boating chores. We watch as one of the guests attempts to sailboard. Again and again, he tries. Again and again, he falls, to the cheers and jeers of people watching him from his boat. At last, he seems able to sail a short distance before losing his balance. He calls for a tow back to the boat. The woman crew comes out in a dinghy to get him and the sailboard. We wonder if perhaps the sailboard effort is a ploy on his part to spend some time with her alone. We hear them chatting on the way back to the sailboat, and it sounds as if this indeed may be the case. Considering his determination with the sailboard, we suspect he may be diligent enough to have some success in the romance department, as well.

At dusk, enjoying our evening drink on the stern, we hear loud braying from the donkey that has been traversing the beach ceaselessly, back and forth, back and forth, since we arrived. Two other donkeys have joined him and he is emoting — *hee-haw, hee-haw, hee-haw.* Perhaps he is pleased, perhaps enraged. Who knows? Donkey communication is not our area of expertise. We have read the park brochure's warning about these wild creatures. They can bite and they can kick — not as cute as they look, it seems.

Abruptly, the braying stops. The two newcomer donkeys disappear into the brush, and our old pal continues his trip back along the beach trail again. Almost at the same moment, a chorus of liquid and musical bird song begins pouring from the forested slopes above the bay. It lasts until the cricket serenade begins at dusk. What a wonderful way to end our day!

...the forested slopes above the bay.

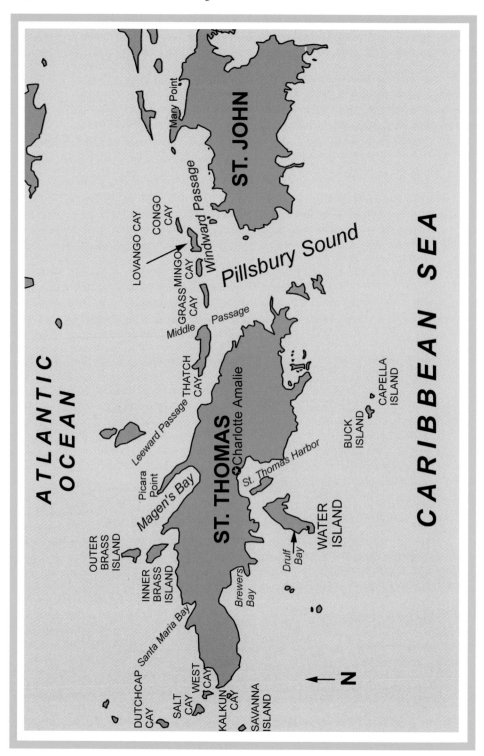

12: Sailing Around St. Thomas

Early the next morning we set out for a sail across Pillsbury Sound and around St. Thomas. We put the sail up, removing the reef from our trip across from St. Croix, and head out of the anchorage around Mary Point, where spindly thatch palms stick up above the trees and bushes like lances. We wonder how

...Mary Point, where spindly thatch palms...stick up like lances.

they survive severe storms. It looks as if they'd snap like matchsticks, but to have grown so tall they must be old, so they have come through some serious gales.

The wind is behind us — our autopilot, familiarly known as Otto, seems incapable of handling the helm, as is usual when we run with wave action. He makes little mincing changes when the situation calls for big swings of the wheel. We discuss newer versions, which we are convinced are a lot more effective than poor Otto.

We are soon at the northern edge of Pillsbury Sound and into the Windward Passage. Everything in the Virgins is so close that it is difficult to have a prolonged sail. To slow our progress a bit, and to improve our view of the islands on this sunny day, we put out only the main, leaving our jib furled.

We pass directly between Congo Cay and Lovango Cay, two long, parallel cays separated by about 500 feet. The water between them is 30 feet deep, but very clear, and we can see the sandy bottom. These are rocky cays with trees and plants struggling to grow in stony crevices.

...these are rocky cays, with trees and plants struggling to grow...

We continue on past a series of skinny cays all lined up lengthwise, east-west. We pass Mingo Cay, Grass Cay, and Thatch Cay. We are gliding slow and silently through the water, at no more than 5 knots. There are no other sailboats, but we do see a couple of small fishing boats. These islands are small, all uninhabited.

...a long line of skinny cays all lined up lengthwise...

Mingo Cay and Thatch Cay are separated by the Middle Passage. Looking through the Middle Passage we see Coral World on the shore of St. Thomas, and many houses on the island's slopes.

We cross the Leeward Passage separating Thatch Cay from St. Thomas, and proceed along the St. Thomas coast. We see Hans Lollik Island off our starboard side. It has a white sand beach lined with palm trees, but we see no sign of habitation. To our port is St. Thomas, with nearly all its steep hillsides spotted with houses.

About halfway down the northern cost of St. Thomas we round Picara Point and sail into Magens Bay. This is a very large bay a couple of miles long and a mile wide that opens to the northwest. It is thus protected from both the east wind and the northern swells. Inside we find calm water 40 or so feet deep. The winds coming down off the mountains all around are gusty. We pull out the jib and tack. For a while we move fast, over 8 knots, then we slow to 3 knots, then the wind shifts. We give it up, drop the main, and motor to the eastern corner of the bay at the north end of the beach. One cruising sailboat is anchored nearby and we see a day-sailor on a mooring, along with many small runabouts. On the beach we see a variety of unmotorized craft, including rowboats, kayaks, sailboards, and small sailboats, all presumably for rent. We anchor in 20 feet of water, over a sandy bottom. The bottom appears to be the same featureless sand everywhere, except for an occasional rock near the shore. The water is clear, and the mile-long beach is packed with people.

...at the eastern end of the beach...

We dinghy ashore for lunch. We pull up our dinghy at the eastern end of the beach and lock it. We walk down the beach past beet-red tourists and pitch-black Islanders, and dozens of young children. The people line the beach, looking for sun, or wade and splash in the clear water. There is no interesting snorkeling here. Any reef-forming organism that takes hold near this shore will soon be trampled or knocked over by many feet.

We have pizza for lunch, and it is delicious. We debate whether this is because we haven't had pizza in so long, or whether this is, in fact, unusually good, but we come to no conclusion.

After lunch we get back into our dinghy and visit the boobies on the rocks off the southernmost end of the beach. We watch in awe as these birds dive into the water at great speeds, with wings tightly closed. They go down quickly and just as quickly, they reappear. These are very athletic birds, fun to watch. They seem quite comfortable with our company and don't fly away even when we approach closely. Perhaps they are used to being watched by people.

Perhaps they are used to being watched by people.

We return to *Top Cat* and continue our circumnavigation of St. Thomas. We put up our mainsail and sail downwind out Magens Bay, where the wreckage of houses on Tropaco Point makes us wonder about the forces (a hurricane, we surmise, with high and breaking waves) that ruined them. We sail be-

...the wreckage of houses on Tropaco Point...

tween Outer Brass Island and Inner Brass Island. These, like all the islands around St. Thomas, are hilly, with rocky cliffs. The protected southwest side of Inner Brass Island has a pretty beach, and we debate whether we could safely anchor off it. We sail into Santa Maria Bay, and survey its two fine beaches. This could be a good anchorage in some conditions, but we suspect there may always be some surge. The problem here is that rollers come in from the north but a boat at anchor will face east into the wind, resulting in continuous rolling.

Looking for an anchorage for the night, we journey on down the coast past some beautiful cliffs, some with huge rocks that slope directly into the sea. At the west end of St. Thomas we round the point into Botany Bay. There is another fine beach here and a large building surrounded by palm trees. But again the bay opens to the north, and we predict a rolly anchorage. We decline to attempt to pass between St. Thomas and West Cay, instead sailing west around a long line of cays and connecting rocks that end with Salt Cay.

The west end of St. Thomas is only lightly populated. All the nearby cays and islands appear to be uninhabited. We pass Dutchcap Cay to our starboard, then as we round Salt Cay, Savana Island and Kalkun Cay. We see no boats, and nobody on any beach or cliff. This trip is strikingly different from our cruises through the British Virgin Islands.

...Salt Cay...

...past some beautiful cliffs...

Shortly after we round Salt Cay we lower our sail and put on the engine. We motor east along the south coast of St. Thomas in a light wind on a quiet sea. We pass more rocky coastline, but no boats.

As we approach the Charlotte Amalie airport we see a couple of boats anchored off Brewers Bay. We continue on to Water Island. Here we find many boats anchored all along the island's western shore. We drop anchor in Drulf Bay, in about 14 feet of water. We see our anchor clearly; it is set well into sand. There is a small beach here, and a number of boats are clearly permanent homes for cruisers.

In the morning we head for Buck Island (yes, this is the second Buck Island we have visited on our trip so far, one of three Buck Islands in the Virgins) and

...Buck Island...

Capella Island, two islands several miles southeast of Charlotte Amalie. The wreck of the *Cartanser Senior* lies off the southwestern shore of Buck Island. There is good diving and snorkeling all around the islands.

We stop at a mooring off the south side of Capella Island. There are several moorings here, all unoccupied. The mooring line we pick up is totally encrusted with barnacles, but appears intact. This is a dive site. We snorkel above it, looking into the deep water. The coral communities slope down from the shore in 20 feet to much deeper water. Below us we see big formations of star coral and staghorn coral, and many seafans. Fish seem to swim at all depths in the 30-foot waters around our boat.

The mooring line...is totally encrusted with barnacles...

We get in the dinghy and explore the two bays off the south and west ends of Buck Island. The first, on the south shore, holds an anchored sailboat. It has a sandy bottom under between 10 and 20 feet of water. The shallows around the shore look like they might offer excellent snorkeling. We continue on to the bay at the west end. A commercial boat full of snorkelers has dropped an anchor very close to the shore. Snorkelers are everywhere. We look for a place to land, but decide not to — there are rocks and corals all alone the edge of the beach. The water is clear and full of life.

The first...holds an anchored sailboat.

It is a very quiet day, with 10 knot winds and little sea. We sail back around 1 o'clock to Charlotte Amalie. Our month-long Virgin Islands vacation is ending. We glide in past the big Marriott Hotel, past scores of boats anchored around the west side of Water Island and in St.Thomas Harbor. There are far fewer boats than when we arrived a month ago. Perhaps the official beginning of hurricane season on June 1 is also the official beginning of the slow season in these waters.

Afterword

We parted at Charlotte Amalie. Nancy returned home by air in a matter of a few hours and David sailed *Top Cat* home, which took a month longer. Our memories of our Virgin Island cruise are very happy ones. The islands are among the most beautiful places we have ever visited by land or sea. They are certainly cruising grounds without peer. We both loved the endless gorgeous beaches of Anegada and the novelty of The Baths and the caves of Norman Island. The beaches, sailing, and snorkeling and diving in the islands are unbeatable. Anchorages there, numerous and delightfully varied in setting, protect well enough to provide a quiet night's sleep. During our visit we had nearly perfect weather and saw very few bugs.

Would we do anything different, if we had it to do over again? Sure. We'd come earlier and stay later. We missed visits to Estate Whim Plantation museum and greathouse and the Cruzan Rum Distillery on St. Croix, a meal at the floating pirate ship restaurant *William Thornton* in Norman Island Bight, a hike through Sage Mountain National Park on Tortola, a visit to Coppermine on Virgin Gorda, to name just a few unrealized opportunities.

But never mind — *we'll be back!*

Index

A

Anegada 59
  Anagada Reef Hotel 66, 77
  Bones Bight 64, 73-74
  Cow Wreck Bay 64, 73
  Dotsy's 69
  Flamingo Bay 72
  Flash of Beauty Restaurant
    and Bar 70
  Keel Point 76
  Loblolly Bay 69, 70
  Pam's Kitchen at the Neptune's
    Treasure Resort 76
  Pomato Point 61-63, 76
  Setting Point 59-60
  Settlement, The 68
  Soldier Point 64
  West End 62, 64, 73
  West End Point 63
  Windlass Bight 64

B

bananaquit 19, 164-165
  nest 32
Beef Island 92
  Long Bay 91
  Trellis Bay 87, 88, 92
Beef Island Channel 92
black-necked stilt 26
Botany Bay 178
brown booby 48, 177

Buck Island, off St.Thomas 180
Buck Island, off Tortola 107-108

C

Cactus Reef 54
Capella Island 182
caves, sea at Norman Island 39-42
climates, Virgin Island **49**
Cockroach Island 99, 101
Colquhoun Reef 54
Columbus, St. Croix landing in 1493
    151, 156
Congo Cay 174
Cooper Island
  Manchioneel Bay 53
Cruising, daily life while
  Energy 13
  Food 12
  Washing up 12
  Waste disposal 13
customs and immigration
  BVI 28-29, 123
  USVI 123

D

Dead Chest Island **52**
Dog Island, near St. Thomas 125
Dog Islands 54, 98-105
donkey 67, 167, 171
Dutchcap Cay 178

Also from Tortuga Books:

Sailing Through Paradise
The Illustrated Adventures
of a Single-handed Sailor

Eager for adventure on the high seas, David Harris left his desk job in March 1998 for a solo sail through the Caribbean. In *Sailing Through Paradise*, Harris takes the reader along on his sometimes exhilarating, occasionally frightening cruise through the West Indies. His delightful writing style enlivens descriptions of his day-to-day experiences while sailing waters around:

- The Bahamas
- The Turks and Caicos
- Hispaniola
- The Virgin Islands
- Puerto Rico

Those who are considering a similar trip will find the book informative. It covers topics of interest such as:

- planning a route
- anchoring and anchorages
- clearing customs
- weather forecasts
- repairs at sea
- cruising equipment

Cruisers who have traveled the Caribbean will enjoy revisiting many spectacular locations through the pages of this book, and for those who only dream of ocean adventure: *Sailing Through Paradise* is dedicated to you.

Sailing Through Paradise is beautifully illustrated with David Harris's spectacular color photographs, and with maps of each leg of his voyage. 224 pages, 151 illustrations, softbound.

$24.95 plus $4.00 shipping and handling.

See instructions for ordering on the next page.